D1613886

Careers in Public Safety:

Cop or Correctional Officer?

Work in Criminal Justice & Make a Difference!

Michael R. Knetzger, Author

M. Louise Damiano, Editor

Jeremy Muraski, Cover Image

First printing, October 2014

ISBN-13: 978-1503117433

ISBN-10: 150311743X

At the time of publication, all hyperlinks and Internet sources were current and contained the properly cited reference material. Internet links and web pages change frequently and the author has no influence or control regarding how or when those links change. Therefore, the reader may not be able to access the recommended or referenced Internet links, web pages or online content. If any Internet links do not work, are "broken" or altered, the reader may conduct an Internet keyword search to help locate the referenced subject matter.

Dedication

This book is dedicated to all present, past, and future police and correctional officers. You have chosen to make great personal sacrifices for fellow man and are protectors of your communities. Never forget why you put the uniform on for the first time and go out each day knowing that *you can make a difference*.

Mike Knetzger

September 2014

Contents

Acknowledgements

Remembering where I came from

When I first set out to become a police officer, like many criminal justice students, I had an idea of what police work was all about. Although my education helped provide insight into the world of law enforcement, two mentors truly taught me what police work was all about. My first ride-along happened in fall of 1990 and it would not have happened without the help of Waukesha County Sheriff's Department Captain (retired) Terry Martorano. Thank you, Captain Martorano, for giving me the opportunity to see police work in the real world. On that first night, I sat next to a former marine, Deputy (retired) Bob Doffek. With my classic hard-rocking shoulder length feathered hair, I looked like I should be in the back seat, not the front. Deputy Doffek greeted me with, "I normally don't like riders, but I'm doing this as a favor for Marty. Just ask good questions." I had no idea what to ask, but apparently I did okay because that first ride along was the beginning of nearly 20 of them with Deputy Doffek who became a friend, mentor, and trainer. Deputy Bob, thank you for taking the time to teach me about fairness, firmness – when necessary, and passion for making a difference in the lives of others. Today, I do what I can to pass on what you instilled to the new generations of police officers.

I'm also grateful to Northeast Wisconsin Technical College (NWTC) Public Safety Dean Elizabeth Paape for always believing in and allowing me to impact criminal justice students in the classroom. Thank you, NWTC Public Safety Coordinator Chris Madson, for the opportunities to instruct, train, and coach police academy students and help prepare them for the real world. To all the Public Safety support staff, thank you for answering the phone when I call – you know I hate voicemail!

I'm also grateful to CTU*online* and Security Studies & Psychology Program Chair David Browne, JD. Thank you for giving me a decade of opportunities to impact thousands of criminal justice students in the online world.

I have also been fortunate to teach in the classroom and online for Rasmussen College. Thank you to Callie Lacy for bringing me on board. Shauna Froelich, your enthusiasm and dedication to your students and making a difference is inspiring. Thank you, Sheriff (Ret) Currie Myers, for the ongoing opportunities with Rasmussen College and allowing me to make a difference in the lives of students.

This book would not have been possible without the support of my very patient and loving wife, Lisa. Thank you for always keeping me grounded and focusing on what is really important. To my children, Madeline and Noah, you inspire me every day to do what I can to make a difference.

To my daughter, Ashley, you will forever be 18 years old. On June 3, 2008, you were taken from us by a drunk driver. Today and forever, Ashley, you will continue to motivate me to do what I can to make a difference in the lives of others and fight for victims. You help me remember where I came from and why I put the uniform on for the first time. If we, the police, don't fight for victims, no one will.

Mike Knetzger

September 2014

About the Author

Mike Knetzger is a 22-year law enforcement veteran and 14-year college instructor with Northeast Wisconsin Technical College (NWTC), Colorado Technical University Online (CTUonline), and Rasmussen College. Mr. Knetzger has had the opportunity to impact thousands of criminal justice students and help them attain their goals of becoming a police or correctional officer. Mr. Knetzger serves as a law enforcement officer, trainer, and SWAT team member with the Green Bay Police Department.

Mr. Knetzger has an Associate of Arts Degree in Criminal Justice from Waukesha County Technical College (1992), a Bachelor of Arts Degree in Justice & Public Policy from Concordia University (1996), and a Master of Arts Degree in Public Administration from the University of Wisconsin – Oshkosh (2000). Mr. Knetzger is a certified State of Wisconsin Technical College Instructor, Unified Tactical Trainer, and certified to teach across the entire criminal justice and tactical curriculum.

Mr. Knetzger has been certified as an expert witness and consulted by district attorneys and police administrators within the state regarding legal, policy and procedure, personnel, and use of force matters. Mr. Knetzger is a sought after public speaker in support of the anti-drunk driving program, "Every 15 Minutes" where he shares the impacting story of his daughter, Ashley, who was killed by a drunk driver. Mr. Knetzger has shared, "Ashley's Story," with over 20,000 high school students, members of the United States Military, law enforcement organizations, and other community groups.

In addition to this book, Mr. Knetzger has co-authored two others books, "True Crime in Titletown, USA ~ Cold Cases" (Badger Books, 2005) and "Investigating High-Tech Crime" (Pearson Education, 2007). Mr. Knetzger has also been published on the nationwide law enforcement website, PoliceOne.

Mr. Knetzger resides in Green Bay, Wisconsin with his wife, Lisa, and their two children, Madeline and Noah.

Introduction

Criminal justice programs across the nation include but aren't limited to courses on criminal and constitutional law, community policing, report writing and community corrections, as well as correctional institutions and administration. Collectively, these studies help prepare students for work in the field. While many students graduate and soon begin applying for police and correctional officer positions, others realize they're intimidated by the extensive hiring processes that identify the best and brightest candidates. Some applicants successfully navigate the process through trial and error, while others are less successful, become discouraged and pursue a different occupation or career.

This book addresses the transition from education to employment. Coupled with your motivation, this book will prepare you to become the best candidate to represent a law enforcement agency or correctional institution. Both career paths have become more complex and demanding over the past several decades; getting hired without a college education has become the exceptional situation. There are increased expectations of those in uniform and it's essential that only the most qualified candidates are hired.

Much of your success in finding a position as a police or correctional officer will hinge on your ability to effectively pass the oral interview. While most candidates are able to pass the written test, too often highly qualified candidates are turned away because they cannot pass the oral interview. In addition to providing an overview of typical criminal justice and corrections hiring practices, the information provided here will offer strategies for success in the oral interview. Often candidates have little to no experience with the oral exam or have not received coaching. Beyond improving your communication skills on the whole with conscious effort and practice, this book will bring you one important step closer to realizing your desired position as a police or correctional officer. In fact, as the author, I confidently offer this guarantee: ***should you not choose to take these guidelines to heart, the success you seek may elude you.***

Chapter 1: Do you have the will to succeed?

Your interest in becoming a police or correctional officer has led you to this book. You're among many who, since September 11, 2001 and the associated wars and conflicts, have contributed to the dramatic rise in criminal justice program enrollments. Television dramas, both reality-based and fictional, have also helped increase enrollments in criminal justice programs. During the recent past, employment in the field has remained steady, even during difficult economic times, and positions in the field are typically considered "secure." Municipalities across the United States are hiring regularly to increase staffing or to offset retirements from the field.

Considerations As You Enter the Criminal Justice or Corrections Field

- While it may be an intrinsically rewarding occupation, you won't get rich serving your community as a police or correctional officer.

   Most people entering the occupation are "service-minded" and want to make a difference while serving others. Beyond this, you are among those who are willing to put yourself in harm's way. Simply put, when citizens call for help in the face of danger, police officers move *toward* it, even at their own peril.

- Both police and corrections occupations are dangerous ones where officers are looking *for*, or are essentially living *with*, dangerous people.

   Corrections officers voluntarily spend eight or more hours per day with dangerous people in jails and prisons. These officers must be mindful of their own safety as well as that of prisoners by using professional communications to maintain order and cooperation, while at the same time promoting rehabilitation.

- The work of police and correctional officers is not as glamorized as popular television shows would have you believe.

   It's rare that police officers are involved in high-adrenaline pursuits to capture the bad guy. This type of call is rare, and often completing the paperwork takes much longer than the incident itself. A good working title for a realistic police show might be "Paperwork Edition"! If you don't like to write, these occupations may not be for you.

- Working conditions in police and correctional fields present unique challenges.

   Among these challenges are long hours, shift work including weekends and holidays, serving those who may not like you (e.g., criminals), average pay, internal and external politics, biohazards, as well as dealing with drug and alcohol abusers. You will also witness tragedy and death resulting from the violence that human beings inflict on one another.

These considerations, over time, may turn your once-healthy or optimistic worldview to a more cynical one, making you a different person than you were before entering the field.

Are you willing to expose yourself to these working conditions? If you answer yes, you're ready to begin considering the knowledge, skills and abilities that form the basis of success in law enforcement and corrections.

Qualities of Successful Police and Correctional Officers

This is not an all-inclusive list, but gives a realistic view of the demands and expectations placed upon police and correctional officers. Now ask yourself, "Am I able to...?"

- Communicate clearly orally and in writing?
- Resolve disputes using professional communications?
- Articulate appropriate law, statutes or ordinances?
- Use appropriate force and arrest people?
- Safely operate a motor vehicle under emergency conditions?
- Apply first aid and take lifesaving measures?
- Explain department policy and procedures?
- Work with little to no supervision?
- Work in a diverse environment with minority group members, physically disabled and mentally ill persons?
- Enforce laws that may conflict with my personal values?
- Testify in court?
- Receive criticism in a professional fashion from fellow officers, supervisors and the general public?
- Be held to higher expectations than the general population as a whole?
- Actively listen, take notes and gather complete information for police reports?
- Effectively resolve and mediate disputes?
- Remain a lifelong learner and complete ongoing training?
- Investigate traffic accidents and enforce traffic laws?
- Counsel children, teens and adults?
- Use critical thinking skills to solve problems?
- Remain fit and maintain a healthy lifestyle?
- Show compassion in making death notifications?
- Continually adjust to the physical and psychological demands of the work?
- Take orders, even if they conflict with my personal values?

If you answered "yes" to any of these questions, then you likely have the will to succeed. If you don't feel you have the necessary knowledge, skills and abilities, are you motivated to find out where and how to gain them?

Don't limit your will to succeed: make it personal. In other words, tie your motivation to something personal that never lets you forget why you want to put the uniform on for the very first time. Following are typical phases of a law enforcement/corrections career and how to best navigate them.

Careers in Law Enforcement and Corrections: The Long View

- Years one to three: The Honeymoon Phase

  Have you ever met a police or correctional officer who was not nervous, excited and proud to put on his/her uniform the first time for the swearing-in ceremony? These officers got the job for all the right reasons. Their personality, character and ethics fit the profile of the ideal officer candidate during the hiring process. They want to help people; they want to make a difference; they enjoy working with people and solving problems. This excitement is maintained throughout field training. Field Training Officers (FTOs) find it refreshing to spend time with officers who genuinely like their jobs. This phase typically lasts one to three years, at which officers begin to realize that the revolving doors of justice continue to allow wrongdoers out time and again. Officers become aware that they respond to the same types of calls each day, sometimes with the same people they arrested the night before. If it's not the same person, it's just a similar call with different people. This phase may give way to burnout.

- Years four to ten: Burnout

  This phase begins when officers who loved coming to work no longer look forward to it. Once willing to work on days off, these officers have tired of working with the "catfish" or "bottom feeders" of society. As mentioned earlier, their worldview has become somewhat cynical, to the point where they may consider all people they help for eight to ten hours per day "catfish." This attitude all too often leads to bitterness, frustration, poor work performance and decision making as well as disciplinary problems from written reprimands to suspensions or termination. Those who persevere through this period enter the Acceptance phase.

- Years ten and beyond: Acceptance

  For some officers, Acceptance is a healthy phase of their career; for others, it becomes a mere ROD (Retired on Duty) existence. In this second group, officers expend the minimum effort to keep supervisors and administration at bay.

Sustaining Career Satisfaction

- Don't lose sight of the universal value, so critical our forefathers included it in The Declaration of Independence: all men [and women] are created equal.

  Police and correctional officers enter the field committing to this value which brings with it the protection and respect for all human life, regardless of sex, race, socioeconomic status, sexual preference and religious beliefs.

  All police and correctional candidates are deemed moral and ethical individuals upon hire. There is a further distinction to be drawn here: moral people recognize wrongdoing, such as stealing or cheating. Ethical people likewise know when they see something wrong, but they are willing to do something about it. This distinction is also what sets police and correctional officers apart from others.

Even when faced with unlawful or dangerous behavior, police and correctional officers must react appropriately within legal as well as ethical guidelines. Reacting with excessive or inappropriate force can result in discipline or even criminal prosecution.

To minimize the risk of burnout, keep the universal value at top of mind. All people have value simply because they are people. If you lose sight of the universal value, you are more likely to use inappropriate communications and excessive force that appears to punish rather than enforce the law you swore to uphold. Reminding yourself of your reason for putting on the uniform will be a strong defense against burnout. See Appendix A for further detail on the universal value.

- Associate and socialize with people outside of your line of work.

There is a special camaraderie in police and correctional work and it's easy to "hang out" with fellow officers. Socializing with your coworkers outside of work blurs the distinction between your work and home life: the conversations are always about something associated with work. Your work friends may also share a cynical worldview, which outside your circle can be perceived as abnormal. You will find it refreshing to socialize with people who are not cops or correctional officers.

- Maintain a sense of humor, healthy eating habits, and get regular exercise.

Police and correctional officers typically have a healthy sense of humor, which serves as a coping mechanism. While some "dark" humor may be viewed as insensitive or inappropriate to others outside the profession, it serves as a buffer to help you cope with many of the tragedies you'll encounter.

The state of hyper-vigilance or heightened state of awareness that enhances survival while on duty may lead to an equal and opposite reaction after work hours. That is, after the pressure is lifted your actions may mimic depression. Typically, after work police and correctional officers prefer to relax and do nothing over discussing their work day with friends or loved ones. This pattern does not bode well for personal relationships, especially when there is withdrawal from loved ones.

This state can be combated with regular cardiovascular exercise. Running, biking, aerobics, or even lifting weights increases the heart rate and also releases dopamine, the chemical in the brain that that creates feelings of happiness.

Finally, healthy eating habits promote a positive self-image and the physiological benefits can't be denied. Avoid processed foods that are typically higher in saturated fat, sodium and cholesterol. Instead, focus on eating natural foods and you'll be much better off. Don't play into the "cop and donut" stereotype!

After reading this first chapter, do you feel police or correctional work is a good fit for you? If not, ***that's OK.*** Now's the time to decide whether police or correctional work is for you, before you invest countless hours in the classroom and several thousand dollars on tuition and fees. If you feel that police or correctional work is for you, then read on and get ready to begin your journey.

Chapter 2: The Criminal Justice Resume

The resume is a critical component of any hiring process. Your resume should demonstrate to the agency that you meet the minimum qualifications and possess the desired knowledge, skills and abilities for the position. A resume should not be longer than one or two pages, with all experience listed in reverse chronological order, i.e., most recent first. If your resume is two pages long, print it on both sides of a single sheet.

Resumes may have any or all of the following elements, in the order set out below. See Figure 1 for a sample resume that includes further detail.

Summary of Qualifications – List three to five bulleted points related to the posted position. Review the agency's job description and create bulleted points that relate your experience with the job requirements.

Education – List all college-level education experiences and degrees. Include the name of the college, cite and state, expected graduation date, name of degree/program, any extracurricular involvement, and your cumulative grade point average (GPA).

Work History – List your three most recent employers. Include your job title, the name of the employer, dates of employment, and two to three bulleted points that describe your primary responsibilities.

Additional Experience – Use this section to highlight your additional experience related to the position. For example, if you've volunteered to provide security at community events while in college, mention this here. Include the name of the organization you volunteered for, the city and state, and the year of the experience.

Specialized Training – You may include this section to document any specialized training you've completed related to the position. For example, you might have attended a one-day seminar on homicide investigation or crime scene processing. Document the name of the specialized training, location and year obtained.

Organizations – In college, you should take the opportunity to become involved in criminal justice-related organizations. A well-known group is the American Criminal Justice Association. Use this section to document your membership in these organizations. Include the name of the organization and years(s) of membership.

Related Skills – In this section, you may describe your skills that are applicable to the position. For example, you could list CPR or first responder certifications, both of which are applicable to the law enforcement and corrections fields.

The sample resume below displays how you might format these elements.

Figure 1 - Sample Resume

SAMANTHA R. JUSTICE
1000 Criminal Justice Way, Green Bay, WI 54301
(920) 445-6623 – Sjustice@email.com

SUMMARY OF QUALIFICATIONS

- Demonstrated knowledge of state traffic and criminal statutes.
- Ability to thoroughly document incidents in writing.
- Ability to use communications skills to resolve conflict.

EDUCATION

Northeast Wisconsin Technical College, Green Bay, WI
Associate of Arts in Criminal Justice – Law Enforcement (GPA 3.5) – May 2014

- Successfully completed Defensive & Arrest Tactics (DAAT), Firearms, Vehicle Contact, Professional Communications, and Emergency Vehicle Operators Course (EVOC)

WORK HISTORY

Security Officer, January 2013 – Present: Justice Hotel & Conference Center, Green Bay, WI

- Responded to and used communications skills to resolve noise complaints.
- Responded to and mediated disturbances or worked with local law enforcement to resolve them.
- Completed written reports of incidents.

Sales Associate – June-December 2012: Correctional Clothing Sales, Green Bay, WI

- Assisted customers with locating and selecting merchandise.
- Created in-store displays to maximize product marketability and appeal.
- Trained new staff members in customer service, marking and money-handling skills.

ADDITIONAL EXPERIENCE

Intern – 2011-2012: Green Bay Police Department, Green Bay, WI

- Participated in 120 hours of ride-along experience on all patrol shifts.
- Observed detectives interview and interrogate suspects.
- Observed crime scene processing and evidence collection.
- Completed a weekly report that summarized all experiences.

Volunteer – 2010-2011: Brown County Fair Security – DePere, WI

- Provided crowd control and safety services for the Brown County Fair attended by approximately 5,000 people.
- Conducted safety checks of the facility including doors, locks, fire exits and fire extinguishers.

ORGANIZATIONS

- Criminal Justice Association – Member (2012-present)
- Alpha Phi Sigma – Honors Criminal Justice Program (2012)
- National Criminal Justice Student Honorary Society (2012)

RELATED SKILLS

- Certified by the National Safety Council in Adult and Infant CPR – 2012 (current)
- Certified by the American Red Cross in First Aid – 2011 (current)
- Proficient in Microsoft Office

References available upon request

When submitting your resume and other application materials, also include a letter of introduction (See Figure 2.) Letters of introduction are often your first chance to "sell" yourself to a potential employer. Your letter should a typed, one-page, error-free document addressed to the contact person, chief of police or jail administrator indicated in the job posting.

The letter should complement your resume and convey why you're qualified for the position. It should also draw attention to the materials you're submitting such as your resume and application materials. Online application processes are becoming more common; you may not have the opportunity to include a letter of introduction. In some cases, however, you'll have the chance to upload attachments with the online application. In contrast, smaller agencies may still use paper-based application processes, which call for properly completed, printed and submitted documents. In these instances, a printed and properly completed application, resume, and letter of introduction will be included.

A professional letter of introduction should contain the following elements:

- Your contact information – Name, mailing address, e-mail address and phone number.
- Date – The date the letter is printed or sent.
- Agency Contact – Include the contact name, if available, title, agency name and method that you are using to send the letter (fax, e-mail, mail).
- Salutation – Whenever possible, address the letter to and individual by name. If no contact name is given, you may use a generic salutation such as "Dear Chief of Police" or "Dear Jail Administrator."
- Introduction – This paragraph should state the title of the position you're applying for, the agency name and how you found out about the position. Continue with a sentence or two that identifies your qualifications for the position. Identify two or three aspects of the position that you're qualified to do.
- Body – Elaborate on your specific knowledge, skills, or abilities that qualify you for the position. Highlight examples from your personal, academic or occupational experiences that make you qualified.
- Conclusion – Summarize what you've already written and outline what is enclosed with the application packet. Close by indicating that you look forward to participating in the hiring process.
- Closing and Signature – Use a simple and standard closing such as "Sincerely" or "Thank you," leave four blank lines for your signature, then type your name below.

Figure 2 – Sample Cover Letter

307 Successful Student Way
Green Bay, WI 54301
January 12, 2014

Ms. Janet Jailer
Jail Administrator
Secure County Jail
2345 Lock Up Drive
Secure, WI 54311

Dear Ms. Jailer:

Enclosed are my completed application materials and resume for the correctional officer position that was announced in the Secure County Gazette. I believe I have the necessary educational, occupational and personal experience to succeed as a correctional officer in your facility.

As a student at Secure County College, I successfully completed all my correctional officer-related coursework with a 3.8 GPA. Much of the coursework was hands-on and I was able to apply the classroom principles to real-world scenarios. For example, in my corrections summary assessment course, I successfully passed all of the scenarios, including the application of professional communications and physical tactics. During my internship with Secure County Jail, I was able to see firsthand how the correctional officers interacted with the inmates and carried out their day-to-day duties.

For the past year, I have worked part-time as a correctional monitor at the Freedom Halfway House. My work at the halfway house has allowed me to interact with inmates who are transitioning from the correctional setting to the community. My interactions have ranged from processing incoming inmates to using my professional communications skills to resolve conflicts or address rule violations. This part-time work has better prepared me for my career goal of becoming a correctional officer.

While in college, I have also had the opportunity to volunteer and make a difference in the community. I have provided 40 hours of volunteer time to the Secure Juvenile Correctional Center where I worked with and developed a fitness program for the juvenile inmates. The juvenile correctional center reported that the juveniles who participated in the fitness program had fewer behavior-related problems than those who did not participate.

I'm confident that my background and experiences will allow me to succeed as a correctional officer in your facility. I look forward to participating in the hiring process. I can be reached at (920) 555-5555 or via e-mail at sandrastone@email.com.

Sincerely,

Sandra Stone

The letter of introduction and resume will often be the first documents the Jail Administrator, Chief of Police or Human Resources Director sees. The quality of your writing and professional tone can positively influence your potential employer while showcasing your ability to communicate in writing. The letter and resume further support the applications materials and help demonstrate that you have the minimum knowledge, skills and abilities to perform the duties of a police or correctional officer. Another way to showcase your qualifications is through a professional portfolio.

Chapter 3: The Portfolio

The professional portfolio is a relatively new concept, especially for criminal justice candidates. Typically, the professional portfolio is compiled in a three-ring binder and contains a complete summary of your personal, occupational and educational successes. Starting your portfolio while still in college will help prepare you for professional work. Keeping the portfolio current is critical and requires a degree of effort. This is also a great place to put certificates of appreciation, certificates of training or awards that help highlight job-related experiences and demonstrate qualifications, knowledge, skills and abilities.

Your professional portfolio should be placed in a new binder and include the following elements:

- **Cover page** on neutral paper bearing your name
- **Table of contents** that reflects the order of tabbed dividers
- **Letter of introduction** submitted with your application packet (If your materials were submitted electronically, here is an opportunity to provide a letter of introduction.)
- **Resume** submitted with your application packet
- **References** – List at least three and no more than five professional references. Avoid using family members or friends as references.
- **Program brochures or summary of degree curriculum** – If available, include a copy of the criminal justice program brochure published by the college. If a program brochure is not available, create a typewritten bullet list of all courses that you have taken within your degree program.
- **Artifacts of competencies attained** – Provide at least one example of exemplary work that you've completed while in college. Since report writing is a necessary skill, a well-written research paper would showcase this skill.
- **Internships** – Include documentation of any internships that you've completed, including summaries of job duties or learning activities that took place over the course of the experience.
- **Additional training** – Include certificates of specialized or additional training that you've received during your college experience and beyond.
- **Volunteer work** – Provide examples or evidence of volunteer work with certificates or letters received from the organizations you've served.
- **Awards** – Include documentation of any awards that you've received.

Use typed divider tabs label and separate each of the elements (see Figure 3).

Figure 3: Sample Professional Portfolio

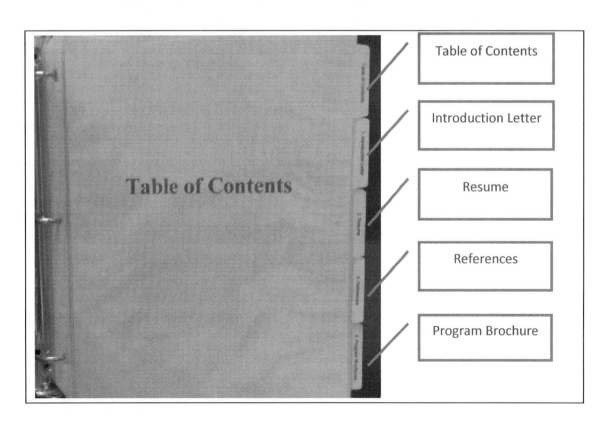

Even if you don't have documentation for each of the elements, it's still a good idea to include tabs for each element within your portfolio. It should be your goal to obtain documentation for each element throughout your college experience and beyond. As you enter your chosen profession, continue to update your professional portfolio. Any time you receive a certificate for specialized training, a letter of commendation or perform additional volunteer work, place this documentation in your portfolio. A current portfolio will be a valuable reference for applying and interviewing for specialty positions or promotional opportunities within your field.

Bring the portfolio with you to any oral board interviews. The extent to which you can use your portfolio during the oral interview will depend upon the rules established by the panel or interviewers. For example, in some municipalities, you cannot show the oral board your portfolio, but you can reference it during the interview. Referencing the portfolio would permit you to open it up and refer to specific contents, such as examples of exemplary work or certificates that you've received. In contrast, if you're interviewing for a position within a small community, you might meet directly with the Chief of Police or Jail Administrator. Either of these individuals may ask to see your portfolio and review it with you. These are great opportunities to "sell" yourself; you shouldn't pass these up.

Electronic portfolios are becoming more common and it's advisable to create one as well. There are many electronic portfolio web sites that you can explore and choose from. One of the more common professional networking and social sites is LinkedIn, which you may use to create an electronic portfolio. LinkedIn is becoming more robust each year and allows you to upload examples of your achievements. The appropriate and professional use of LinkedIn and other social media web sites may affect your chances of landing a position. Surveys show that 85 percent of hiring managers say a candidate's positive digital presences influenced their hiring decisions (Boudreaux, 2012). It's common for police and correctional agencies to conduct Internet searches and checks of potential candidates and even current employees. Therefore, it's also ideal for you to check your own name on the Internet at least twice per year to view the results. After all, you should see what potential employers will. This is also a great reason to keep your Internet presence professional and appropriate. Don't post images or comments that you might later regret.

The portfolio is a valuable piece that can help you obtain a position and later advance in your career. Keep your portfolio current as you attain additional training, education and experience. Even though your agency should keep good records related to your ongoing professional development, it's essential that you keep your own documentation as well. After all, the person that should be most concerned about your career, lifelong learning and success is *you!*

Once you've completed your letter of introduction, resume and portfolio, you're truly prepared to begin applying for police or correctional officer positions. Before we turn our attention to the rest of the hiring process, it's important to become familiar with the unique work environments that you'll encounter. Familiarity with the police and correctional work environments will help you better understand common pay scales, organizational structures, the role of unions, and how discipline is carried out.

Chapter 4: The Work Environment

Functioning well in police and correctional environments means maintaining realistic expectations. Until well into your career, the hours won't be "normal" and you'll be expected to cover afternoon and night shifts. You'll work weekends and holidays. If you can't get vacation time off, you'll likely work on other important days in your life such as children's birthdays and anniversaries. You'll work 8- to 12-hour shifts and be required to attend mandatory training, court appearances during time off, and may be called in to work when staffing is short.

While wages have improved over the years, you won't become "rich." Wage levels vary across the nation, with the average starting salary being $38,000 per year, not including overtime and holiday pay. Starting wages are typically higher in the Midwest and West Coast and lower in the southern and eastern states. Salaries increase as officers progress through rank. (See Tables 1 and 2 for sample police and correctional officer salary schedules.)

Table 1 - Occupational Employment and Wages for Police and Sheriff's Patrol Officers

Industry/Position	Hourly Mean Wage	Annual Mean Salary
Local Government (City, Town, Village Police)	$27.73	$57.670
State Government (Troopers, Criminal Investigators)	$30.20	$62,810
Federal Executive Branch (FBI, DEA, Secret Service)	$25.30	$52,620
Colleges and Universities (Campus Police)	$23.32	$48,500

**Source: Bureau of Labor Statistics, Occupational Employment and Wages, May 2012

Table 2 - Occupational Employment and Wages for Correctional Officers and Jailers

Industry/Position	Hourly Mean Wage	Annual Mean Salary
Local Government (Jailers)	$20.50	$42,650
State Government (Correctional Officers)	$21.23	$44,180
Federal Executive Branch (Federal Correctional Officers)	$25.67	$53,400

*Source: Bureau of Labor Statistics, Occupational Employment and Wages, May 2012

Law Enforcement Organizational Structure

All police departments and correctional facilities operate under a paramilitary structure; the rank and file system is similar to the structure of the military. The paramilitary structures are hierarchical in nature where communication flows from the bottom up and top down. The hierarchy also clearly defines the levels of authority and management that all officers are expected to follow. This is also referred to as the "chain of command." Officers are expected to respect the chain of command and take their concerns to their immediate supervisor, typically a member of middle management such as a Corporal or Sergeant. The middle manager is responsible for making the appropriate decision and/or taking the issue to the next level of management. See Figure 4 for an overview of the typical hierarchical structure.

Figure 4 – Common Police Department Hierarchical Structure

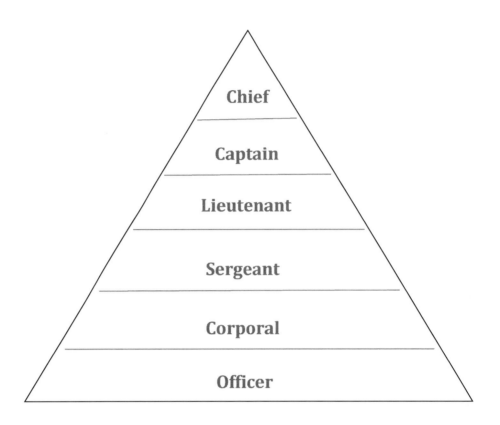

Each position in the paramilitary hierarchy of a police organizational structure is set out below. The size of the agency and related organizational mode will determine levels within the organization. For example, some agencies prefer a "flatter" organizational model with fewer levels of management, which may not include corporals or sergeants. Other organizational models are more robust and could contain all the levels shown in Figure 4.

The Chief is the leader of the police organization who reports directly to the leader of the municipality (e.g., mayor, city manager, village president, or town board president) along with the police and fire commission. The chief of police is responsible for all facets of the organization including the direction, planning, budgeting, hiring and termination of officers. The success of the chief depends to a great degree upon the performance of officers in supporting positions.

The Captain is a division leader who supervises sworn and non-sworn personnel and plans and coordinates the operations of a division, whether it is a detective, patrol or support service division. This individual also ensures that each division or shift within the division is adequately staffed. Reporting directly to the Chief of Police, the Captain also participates in planning, budgeting and setting goals for the division. In the absence of the chief of Police, the Captain may be considered acting chief.

The Lieutenant is a division supervisor (e.g., administration, patrol, booking) who receives general direction from a captain or chief. This individual has direct supervision over sworn and non-sworn personnel. The Lieutenant evaluates officers' work, conducts studies, reads/reviews reports, ensures cooperative working relationships among divisions and may initiate personnel investigations. This position reports directly to the Captain.

The Sergeant is a direct field supervision assigned to a shift. Often referred to as a "working supervisor," when this individual is not supervising, he/she is taking calls for service, booking prisoners and participating in the day-to-day work with officers. The Sergeant may also review reports, make suggestions for follow-up or corrections, or train new officers. Finally, the Sergeant may refer disciplinary matters to a lieutenant for appropriate follow-up and action. The Sergeant reports directly to the Lieutenant.

The role of **the Corporal** is similar to that of an officer, but he/she may have some additional duties to act as a supervisor in the absence of a sergeant. Corporals are often the most senior officers on a particular shift and bring the necessary field experience and specialized knowledge to the field. This allows them to make decisions in the absence of a supervisor. Corporals are not formally considered supervisors and cannot enact disciplinary procedures. The Corporal reports directly to the Sergeant.

Patrol Officers are the "backbone" of any agency. They are the first interaction citizens have with police or correctional facilities. The perceived nature of this first contact, most influenced by professional communications skills, will determine how well situations will be resolved. These officers do the work in the field and are most responsible for bringing law violators to justice. The Patrol Officer reports directly to his/her assigned Corporal or Sergeant.

Correctional Facility Organizational Structure

The organizational structure of a correctional facility is similar to that of a police department and also has a hierarchy or "chain of command" that you're expected to follow. Inside these institutions, the ranks of officer, corporal, sergeant, lieutenant and captain are typically the same. However, the leader of a correctional institution is usually referred to as the Warden or Correctional Administrator and not a Chief of Police. Some jails may not have anyone in these roles, and in those instances, the top administrator is the Sheriff.

Benefiting From the Experience of Others

Take advantage of the knowledge and experience of your supervisors. You are also expected to follow the policies and procedures established by the department. If you're unsure how to handle a certain task, ask for help! It's better to ask for help and handle things correctly the first time than to make the wrong decision or take the incorrect action. Mistakes in some businesses might result in loss of profit. However, mistakes in police or correctional work may result not only in the miscarriage of justice, but termination of your employment, or even worse, civil or criminal action. Most experienced officers will report that it took them at least three years to become completely comfortable and confident in the field. Until that time, don't hesitate to rely on those who have come before you.

In addition to being familiar with the chain of command, it's also essential that you know the rights afforded to you as a police or correctional officer. These employment rights are dictated by the laws set up within each state and are carried out or managed by a union.

It's common for police and correctional officers to have some sort of union representation that helps monitor the work environment and protect employee rights. The extent of union representation and influence is dependent upon the state where you work. There are two types of union-related working environments in the United States: **right-to-work states** and **collective bargaining states**. You should become familiar with each type of working environment.

In right-to-work states, the law protects employees from being forced to join or financially support a union. Therefore, if you're hired by a police department or correctional institution that is represented by a union, you have the choice to join the union and pay dues or refuse. If you choose not to join the union, however, you can still benefit from the services and conditions that the union helped establish. The union is also still required to represent you in any disciplinary matters, up to and including termination proceedings.

In contrast, if you work in a *collective bargaining state*, all police and correctional officers represented by the union must pay union dues. Although the differences between right to work and collective bargaining may appear slight on the surface, they are significant:

In a collective bargaining environment, laws typically require the union and the municipality (represented by police management) to bargain and agree on most matters related to *wages, hours, and working conditions*. Members of the union elect representatives who comprise the union board. It's common for the union board to include representatives from each shift—days, afternoons and nights—and specialized divisions such as detectives or school resource officers. This helps ensure that issues unique to each job function are addressed during negotiations. This allows for a union representative to be present regularly to monitor the work environment, field operations, address contractual questions and to identify or respond to violations of the contractual agreement. Both sides also have legal counsel available to them who are either present during negotiations or who review all agreements before they are signed.

Topics related to *wages* include the following:

- Officers' salaries
- Overtime
- Holiday pay
- Shift differential pay
- Other financial incentives such as physical fitness or field training officer pay.

Discussions related to *hours* often include the officers' hourly work schedule or shift assignments. The evaluation of *working conditions* has a broader scope, and may include

- how specialty positions such as SWAT or dive team are obtained,
- the process for promotions and determination of minimum qualifications,
- how shift assignments are made, and
- disciplinary processes.

A further distinction between right-to-work and collective bargaining states is the scope of permitted bargaining. In a right-to-work environment, permitted bargaining is more restrictive and the municipality is required only to "meet and confer" and bargain fairly on certain issues. For example, a municipality may be required only to bargain issues related to salary, but hours and working conditions are exclusively managed by administration; in other words, they are management rights. The issues that must be bargained and those that are considered "management rights" vary from state to state. In a right-to-work state, management is often required to "meet and confer" and bargain fairly on those issues of management rights, but have the ultimate say. Some of those management rights can have a significant effect on your day-to-day life, such as the hours you are to report to duty. For example, although you may be assigned to the afternoon shift, if the agency determines a staffing need on the night shift the next day, you may be required to work night shift the next night and then back to the afternoon shift the following day. Such an inconsistent schedule can wreak havoc on your personal and family life. In a collective bargaining environment, on the other hand, this is often prevented because the agency is required to pay overtime, call-in pay or premium pay for changing an officer's work schedule.

Drawing up a Contract

When an agreement is reached between the union and the municipality, it is documented in a contact. Once representatives of the union and the municipality sign the contract, it then becomes a legally binding agreement. Again, the extent or scope of what is legally binding varies from state to state. Most contractual agreements span a three-year period and are then renegotiated. Negotiations typically begin before the current contract expires. If a new agreement is not reached before the current one expires, the current contract remains in effect until a new one is settled.

Grievance Procedures

The contract serves as the primary legal document that establishes the framework and agreement between management and labor. Violations of the contract are resolved by a formal process known as a grievance procedure.

For example, suppose there is a contractual rule that requires overtime slots in the patrol division to be filled by seniority with the most senior officer being offered the slot before less senior officers. If an officer with less experience or time on patrol is offered the slot before an officer with more experience or time on patrol, this constitutes a violation of the contract. To rectify this violation, the senior patrol officer would first bring it to the attention of his/her union representative. The union representative would gather the facts necessary to investigate and substantiate the violation. Once substantiated, the union representative would file a formal notice, usually in writing, to the administration advising them of the violation.

The administration typically has seven to ten days to respond to the allegation. The administration can either reject the allegation or acknowledge it and offer a solution. One solution might be to allow the most senior officer (who should have been offered the overtime) to work it at another time. If the administration rejects the claim, then the formal grievance process continues. In most states that recognize contractual rights, the grievance process contains the following steps:

- Identifying a violation of the collective bargaining contract
- Gathering information to substantiate the violation
- Presenting the violation to management, who may either resolve or reject it
- Referring rejected complaints to the Police & Fire Commission (PFC), who may resolve or reject it (Complaints that reach the PFC are typically rejected in support of the police administration.)
- Forwarding complaints rejected by both management and the PFC to a state-appointed arbitrator for mediation to avoid the cost of litigation or a quasi-judicial hearing before an arbitrator (All decisions of the arbitrator are final and binding.)

A Collective Voice

The main reason for having a union is to provide a collective voice that aims to create a level playing field for wages, hours, and working conditions as well as disciplinary procedures, protections and processes. Unions are intended to create an environment free of favoritism and nepotism, where "side deals" cannot be reached for better positions or reduced accountability due to personal relationships.

Oftentimes, however, a strong collective bargaining agreement may create an environment where officers who perform poorly or make poor off-duty lifestyle choices are protected. At the same time, it's imperative that all officers--regardless of personality, personal friendships, or questionable actions—have the same protections and due process rights to protect their employment status.

Without these fair and consistent processes or procedures, others may assume that certain officers, such as those who enjoy a friendship with the chief, might get preferential treatment over other officers who are outspoken or may disagree with managerial or organizational decisions.

Fair Discipline

Another important responsibility of the union is ensuring that discipline is meted out fairly and consistently, in keeping with the contractual agreement. Most police and correctional agencies follow a progress discipline model. The progressive discipline model allows for discipline to begin with oral and written reprimands up to and including suspensions and terminations. For example, officers late for roll call will likely be given an oral reprimand. Being late a second time a few months later will likely result in a written reprimand. If similar performance problems continue, a paid or unpaid suspension may be issued; termination is also a possible outcome. This is a generalization and isn't necessarily followed in all cases. However, if an officer commits a serious policy and procedure violation such as intentional and excessive force or perjury, he/she may be suspended or even terminated for the first occurrence.

Unions and the New Officer

Once hired, you'll serve a probationary period, which typically lasts 12 to 18 months. During this period, you're considered an **at-will** employee and can be terminated without cause. To avoid allegations of discrimination on the part of the agency, probationary employees are typically terminated *with* cause, often during the field training period where an inability to perform the necessary job functions becomes obvious.

Once you've completed your probationary period, however, you're no longer considered an at-will employee and you have a **property right** to your position. This property right, once earned, requires due process before it can be taken away. This is the primary reason for a progressive discipline structure and a quasi-judicial process that applies when suspending or terminating a police officer.

Similar to the grievance process, when a violation of policy, procedure, or state or federal law has been alleged, an investigation is begun. Depending on the size of the agency, the investigation will be conducted by a supervisor or a member of an internal affairs division. During the course of the investigation, the officer is questioned about the behavior or the allegations. During questioning, officers typically have the right to legal counsel and/or the presence of a union representative to ensure that established processes are properly followed.

Before questioning begins, the officer may be advised of his/her "Garrity Rights," which were established by the U.S. Supreme Court case of Garrity v. New Jersey (1967) as summarized below.

In 1961, the New Jersey Supreme Court ordered the State Attorney General to investigate an alleged "ticket fixing" scheme occurring in two different townships. Six police officers, including Police Chief Edward Garrity, were under suspicion and questioned. At the time of questioning, the officers were advised that anything they said could be used in a criminal proceeding; that they had the right to refuse answering self-incriminating questions; and that a refusal to answer questions would be cause for termination. All of the officers answered questions and some of their answers were used, over their objections, in criminal proceedings against them. They were convicted of conspiracy to obstruct the administration of traffic laws; the decision was ultimately upheld by the New Jersey Supreme Court. They appealed to the U.S. Supreme Court and their convictions were overturned for the following reasons:

- The threat of termination rendered any statements involuntary and, therefore, inadmissible in state criminal proceedings.
- The choice to be terminated or self-incriminate constituted coercion.
- The option to lose their livelihood (i.e., be terminated) or self-incriminate is contrary to the idea of the free choice to speak or to remain silent.
- Police officers are not relegated to a "watered-down" version of constitutional rights.

Today, prior to questioning that may result in discipline (i.e., written and permanent personnel file entry), suspension or termination, officers are first advised of the nature of the questioning and the following Garrity Rights:

- You have the right to be informed of the allegations involved.
- You will be asked questions specifically directed and narrowly related to the performance of your official duties.
- Statements made during any interviews may be used as evidence of misconduct or as the basis for seeking disciplinary action against you.
- Any statements made by you during these interviews cannot be used against you in any subsequent criminal proceedings, nor can the fruits of any of your statements be used against you in any subsequent criminal proceeding.
- If you so request, a person of your choice may be present to serve as a witness during the interviews (www.garrityrights.org).

Questioning begins after the Garrity Rights advisement and officers are expected to answer questions truthfully and honestly. Answers can be used against an officer in any subsequent disciplinary action, up to and including termination. The results of the interview become part of the entire investigation into the alleged wrongdoing. If a police or correctional agency moves for termination, officers may either accept the termination and/or exercise their right to have a quasi-judicial hearing in front of a police or fire commission (PFC) who will then decide the case. It is referred to as a "quasi-judicial process" because, like a criminal court hearing, a termination hearing affords the right to counsel, the right to present witnesses on the officer's behalf, and the right to cross-examine witnesses brought against the officer. The decision of the PFC is final, but it can be appealed to district or circuit court where a judge will then review the case *on the record* (that is, examine the transcript of the PFC hearing and render his/her decision). If the judge's decision is contested, it can be brought to an appeals court for review. The appeals court would likely be the final step unless there is a significant constitutional issue that could cause the State or U.S. Supreme Court to accept and hear the case, which is precisely what happened in Garrity.

It's not uncommon for an agency to have more than one union. For example, in a larger agency, such as the Los Angeles Police Department, there is a patrol officers' union, sergeants' union, and supervisory unions. Upon entering law enforcement, depending upon the state where you work, you'll discover the type of union representation afforded to you. Make a point of becoming familiar with your contractual rights and protections.

Once you've been hired by a police agency that has some sort of union organization, you should be approached by a union representative regarding the cost, benefits, and protections that are afforded to you. It's also likely that you will not be afforded full union protections until you have completed your training and/or probationary period. It's important to find out when your union benefits and protections are in full effect.

In summary, union representation is an important concept and it's critical that you become aware of the type of union environment you will be entering. Become familiar with the rights afforded to you and hope that you will not need to exercise them, especially in cases of alleged wrongdoing. Remember, as a probationary officer you are not afforded many rights, if any, and are considered an at-will employee who can be terminated without cause. Termination without cause rarely happens and agencies will often do all they can to keep you because of the significant time and money they've invested in you. The cause for termination is most often documented during the field training period. This is all the more reason to take your training and probationary period seriously. Once off probation, you will have the full protections and benefits of the union. However, even the best union protections cannot stop unethical police and correctional officers from eventually finding themselves in trouble and facing termination or even legal sanctions. Continue to be an ethical police or correctional officer and *you should never need union protections.*

Chapter 5: The Criminal Justice Hiring Process

The criminal justice hiring process is extensive and can also be intimidating, especially when you don't really know what to expect. However, a thorough process is necessary to identify the most qualified and ethical candidates for a limited number of positions. The hiring process used by police departments and correctional facilities varies across the country. Typically, the larger the police department or correctional facility, the longer the process takes. The depth and length of the process depends upon many factors such as the number of applicants, the number of open positions, the minimum requirements, and the steps in the process deemed necessary by the agency. Below are the various steps of a typical criminal justice hiring process. The order in which it is completed will ultimately be determined by the police agency or correctional facility.

- Step 1 - Written application
- Step 2 - Written test or assessment center
- Step 3 - Screening interview
- Step 4 - Physical agility
- Step 5 - Full panel interview
- Step 6 - Ranking of successful candidates
- Step 7 - Background investigation
- Step 8 - Conditional job offer (polygraph examination, psychological screening, medical screening)
- Step 9 - Official job offer with starting date

Step 1 – Written Application

The written application is the first and most basic part of the process. It may seem like common sense, but it's essential that you properly complete the written application, consistent with the standards established by the agency. Unfortunately, candidates are sometimes rejected simply because the application is not completed exactly as directed. Others do not meet the minimum qualifications (e.g., age, level of education, experience) and are eliminated from the process as well.

All police and correctional officer applications have specific instructions regarding completion. You must pay close attention to the instructions, including deadlines for filing it with the appropriate human resources division or department, and where to mail and/or deliver it in person. Incomplete or improperly completed applications will likely be rejected. For example, the Orlando, Florida Police Department recruitment Web page clearly states, "Anyone submitting an incomplete application will not be invited to attend the civil service exam." (Orlando Police Department, 2010).

Unless directed otherwise, complete all fields/blanks on the application. If certain fields or parts of the application do not apply to you, simply put "N/A" (Not Applicable) in that field. A carefully completed application demonstrates your ability to follow instructions and pride of workmanship. It is also important to write legibly or type the application. Some applications are available online and can be filled out and submitted via the Internet. Other agencies may still use paper applications, which require handwritten or typed responses. If you properly complete the application and meet the minimum requirements, you will move onto the next step of the process. In most cases, you will be notified in writing via mail or email if you have successfully passed this step and advised where to appear for the written test and/or assessment center.

Keep in mind that the application will, sometimes several months later, be viewed by background investigators. Your application forms the basis of the background investigation later in the process. As you progress through the hiring process, if any of the information contained within the application has changed, such as new employer information, update the agency with the new details.

Assuming you've successfully completed the written application and meet the minimum qualifications for the position, you'll then take the written test and/or participate in what is referred to as an assessment center.

Step 2 – Written Test and/or Assessment Center

Most police departments and correctional facilities will administer a written test and/or an assessment center for all applicants who successfully complete the application process.

The content and format of the written test vary across the country. The written test is often referred to as a "Civil Service Exam." A civil service exam is a written test that has been created, endorsed or approved by a state standards board or agency and can be used by municipalities within the state. Municipalities may also create and administer their own written tests and/or hire a company to create and administer one for them. The written tests typically evaluate basic reading comprehension and math skills, writing and English language skills, recollection and deduction abilities, and knowledge of laws or principles related to law enforcement or corrections. The test format includes multiple choice questions, short answer or essay responses, and fill-in-the-blank items. Some agencies provide a study booklet outlining the subject areas on the test and some sample questions. There are also many self-help resources available in print and on the Internet. Some of the well-known prep books that include practice tests include:

- *Master the Police Officer Exam* and *Master the Correctional Officer Exam: Take the next step toward a Career as a Corrections Officer* (published by ARCO)
- *Police Officer Exam* and *Corrections Officer Exam* (published by Learning Express)
- *Barron's Police Officer Exam* and *Barron's Correction Officer Exam* (published by Barron's)

Because it can be difficult to predict exactly what will be on a civil service exam, it's important to take as many practice tests as possible.

A typical criticism of written tests is that they are merely academic and measure only rote learning, or memorization, rather than your potential success as a police or correctional officer. The assessment center approach is designed to address this criticism; more police and correctional agencies are using this approach.

Assessment centers comprise a series of active, hands-on assessments, and provide another way to test or evaluate how well you integrate and apply knowledge, skills, and abilities in law enforcement or corrections. Assessment centers have become increasingly common in the past decade and allow for more accurate evaluation of your abilities to carry out the necessary functions of a police or correctional officer. Assessment centers provide an opportunity to demonstrate your comprehension and application of tactical skills, interpersonal skills, leadership skills, communication and presentation skills, observation and recollection skills, and written communications skills.

Assessment centers can have multiple segments, including a written exercise, structured interview, oral presentation, observation and recollection exercise, search exercise, and an inventory exercise. Below are some examples of assessment center exercises that have been used by police agencies.

- **The Round Table:** In this exercise, two or three candidates are brought into a room and seated at a table. All candidates are given the same topic, such as community policing, and are asked to apply community policing principles to a specific problem. The candidates will have approximately ten minutes to study the problem and come up with a three-minute presentation that addresses the problem with community policing principles. Each candidate will then make a presentation to the other candidate(s) and any evaluators present. This exercise evaluates communications skills, critical thinking, application of police/academic principles to the real world, and the ability to explain how the candidate would solve the problem.
- **Report Writing:** Candidates will view a crime in progress video. Candidates will see the video one time and be able to take notes regarding what they see. Candidates will then be asked to complete a police report narrative. This exercise evaluates a candidate's ability to note important details such as suspect or vehicle descriptions, license plate numbers or evidence, and use the notes to compose a police report narrative. The report narratives are evaluated for grammar and content.
- **Crime in Progress:** Candidates will be shown a crime in progress video one time and then be asked to orally recollect important details related to the crime in progress. This evaluates the candidate's ability to remember and recollect the most important details of a crime in progress, such as license plate numbers, physical descriptions or names, directions of travel, and descriptions of weapons.
- **The Vehicle Inspection:** Candidates will have an allotted period of time (e.g., five minutes) to examine a vehicle that has been impounded at the police department. Candidates are permitted to take notes during this exercise. Candidates will then be asked a series of questions related to the vehicle and its contents. This exercise evaluates a candidate's ability to search a vehicle, identify and evaluate evidence, conduct a proper inventory, locate and document evidence, note a vehicle license plate number, and vehicle identification number, color, make, and model.

Passing the written test and/or assessment center is critical to your success. If you do not pass either of them, you will not continue in the process. Unfortunately, if you don't pass, the agency is not obligated to tell you exactly why and will not offer feedback. Trial, error, and failure are unfortunately part of getting better. You can increase your chance of success by being properly prepared and using the recommended resources in this section.

Step 3 - Screening Interviews & Full-Panel Interviews

The screening interview and full-panel interviews are considered separate steps in some hiring processes. Since success strategies for both are similar, they are both discussed here.

Screening Interviews

The screening interview is often used by agencies that have a larger applicant pool (in excess of 100); smaller agencies may skip this step. A screening interview is shorter than a full-panel interview. A screening interview usually lasts fewer than ten minutes, consists of approximately three or four questions, and is administered by two or three officers or supervisors representing the police or correctional agency. Questions asked during a screening interview are often related to why you want to be a police or correctional officer for the agency, along with your qualifications, experience, and education. A scenario-based question may also be asked. Two common screening interview questions are:

- Why do you want to be a police or correctional officer for our agency?
- What have you done to prepare yourself for the position of police or correctional officer?

Best practices and recommendations regarding how to answer these questions are discussed later in this chapter.

Full-Panel Interviews

In contrast, a full-panel interview usually lasts approximately 20 minutes, consists of five or more questions, and is administered by a five- to seven-member panel. The evaluators for the full-panel police officer interview often comprise members of the police department, the municipal leader (mayor, village president, or town chairman) or county leader (county executive), a member(s) of the police & fire commission, and a member(s) of the community. Evaluators of a correctional officer interview panel may include the jail or prison administrator, supervisors, correctional officer, and a person from the county or state human resources division.

A diverse board of evaluators allows for multiple perspectives and a more accurate assessment of your knowledge, skills, and abilities to perform the necessary functions of the position. The types of questions asked are similar to the screening interview questions mentioned above, as well as various other questions, and scenario-based questions. See Appendix B contains a complete list of potential oral interview questions.

The Interview Environment

The interview environment is intimidating by design, with the evaluators seated at a long table with you seated on a chair in front of them (See Figure 5). This type of interview environment allows evaluators to see how well you think under stress.

Figure 5 – Sample Oral Interview Environment

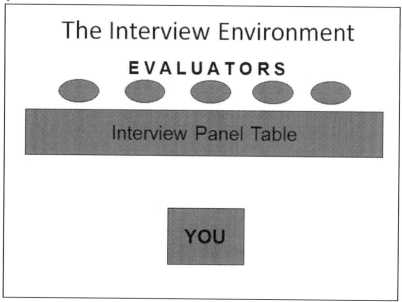

There's often a time limit of two to three minutes to answer each question. Two to three minutes may seem like a long time to talk about yourself, especially under stress, and in front of evaluators you don't know. Nonetheless, it's beneficial to use the allotted time. Applying the three-step process or "road map" discussed later in this chapter to most of the questions you'll be asked in an oral interview will help develop a complete and professional response.

Preparing for the Interview

Make sure you arrive on time for your interview. Try to arrive at least 15 minutes early. Don't be surprised if you find yourself waiting past your assigned time. There are typically several candidates scheduled on the same day and the intensive interview process often gets behind schedule.

"Dressing for success" applies to the oral interview environment. Dress should be "business professional" for both men and women. Some larger agencies might have the written test, screening interview, and physical agility test in the same day or over a span of two days.

This may require you to bring appropriate clothing for each step:

- For men, acceptable dress includes a matching long-sleeved shirt and tie, suit coat, dress pants, and matching socks and shoes. Men should also be well groomed, including facial hair, or be clean shaven.
- For women, acceptable dress includes a matching blouse, blazer, dress slacks or knee-length skirt, socks and shoes or heels that are lower than two inches. For women, a good general rule to follow is, "If you would wear it to a club, than you shouldn't wear it to an interview."

Both men and women should choose dark, conservative colors (e.g., navy, dark gray or black) and all attire should be clean and well pressed.

Tattoos and Jewelry

It's important to keep in mind the policies and procedures of the agencies that you're applying for. Many agencies will not permit you to have visible tattoos and male officers are often prohibited from wearing any jewelry except rings. Visible tattoos may also be negatively perceived by the interview panel. It is best to cover all potentially visible tattoos. All candidates should avoid excessive jewelry. Male candidates should remove all jewelry except wedding bands or rings. A pair of earrings is acceptable for female candidates. Other piercings should be removed for the interview. It's unlikely that nose, lip, or eyebrow piercings would be permitted by agency policy and would have to be removed upon hire or not worn while on duty.

Business professional attire and appearance for female candidates:

- Solid color suit coat (navy blue, black, or dark gray)
- Matching blouse
- Matching dress pants
- Matching shoes
- Limited jewelry
- Professional hairstyle
- Neatly manicured, clean nails
- Light makeup and perfume
- No visible tattoos

Business professional attire and appearance for male candidates:

- Solid color suit coat (navy blue, black, or dark gray)
- Matching dress shirt
- Matching dress pants
- Conservative tie
- Matching shoes
- Limited jewelry
- Professional hairstyle
- Clean shaven
- Neatly manicured, clean nails
- Light cologne
- No visible tattoos

The Oral Interview

Your full name is eliminated from all paperwork to help keep the interview as unbiased as possible. You'll likely be introduced to the interview panel with an assigned number or by your first name and last initial. It's appropriate to shake hands with each evaluator and provide a welcoming comment such as, "It's nice to meet you." Have a seat when you're directed to do so. Make sure all electronic devices are put away, set to silent, or turned off. If you brought your portfolio, set it on the table in front of you, but keep it closed. The evaluators may ask to see your portfolio or inquire about it. This is a perfect opportunity to explain that it contains a complete summary of your occupational, educational, and personal successes and that they are welcome to review it. If the evaluators accept your offer, present it to them and return to your chair. As mentioned earlier, they may also tell you that they aren't permitted to view it, but that you may reference it during the oral interview. The portfolio contains a wealth of supporting information that you can refer to when responding to questions such as, "What have you done to prepare yourself for the position of police/correctional officer?"

One panel member often manages the interview and will explain the process to you, such as the number of questions that you'll be asked and any time limits for each answer. They may ask if you have any questions about the interview format. Don't hesitate to ask questions if necessary. Listen to each question and pause a moment to collect your thoughts before answering. Taking a deep breath and thinking through your answer before speaking will help you formulate a more complete response.

Body language, posture, speaking style, ability, and skill are important aspects of an oral interview to be aware of and are coincidentally important to your success as a police or correctional officer as well. While seated, maintain an upright and open posture. Don't slouch or cross your arms. Slouching creates an image of disinterest and crossing your arms is often regarded as a closed or guarded posture. Rest your hands comfortably on your lap or on the table in front of you and be prepared to gesture while answering the questions. Use your hands to emphasize points that you want to make. It's also appropriate to lean forward while speaking and address all members of the panel by making eye contact. Don't just focus on the evaluator who asked the question, but rather scan the entire panel.

Speaking style, ability, and skill are critical for oral interview success. You may be gifted with dynamic speaking abilities while others have to work at it. A common speaking mistake during oral interviews is the use of "fillers" when answering questions. Common fillers are "er," "um," or "ah" and have no meaning. Other fillers include the redundant use of "like" and "you know" while speaking. Fillers convey a message of uncertainty, nervousness, lack of confidence, or that you're "thinking aloud." A filler is often used in a sentence when a speaker is unsure of what to say next. For example, "I want to be a police officer, ah, because I want to, um, work with people and, ah, make a difference." The fillers (ah and um) lessen the credibility of the candidate's motive for wanting to become a police officer. Fillers also convey a lack of confidence on the part of the speaker.

Unfortunately, fillers have become all too common in everyday conversation and conscious effort is necessary to avoid them. If they are common in your everyday speech, they will become more pronounced during your stressful oral interview. Breaking these bad habits requires being aware of them and mindfully eliminating them from your everyday speech. Like any skill, it's important to "practice the way you play" and that includes how you speak. Work at removing unnecessary fillers from your everyday speech.

Instead of using a filler while gathering your thoughts, just remain silent. A brief silent pause is often interpreted as "thinking" and is considered a more professional and intelligent approach. Many people are uncomfortable with silence, especially when the audience is focused on them. However, silence makes for an improved response. Silence can improve focus on your response, while fillers often interfere with the thought process.

Tone and pace are other important aspects of effective communication. Think of the best presenters or instructors you've seen. How did they communicate? Successful presenters or instructors often show passion and energy in the way they present. Now think of instructors who put you to sleep. They likely used a monotone voice. Your tone should convey your sincerity, motivation, and convictions. If you're a fast talker by nature, nervousness will often increase pace and using effective pauses (explained above) can help you slow down. You can practice tone and pace with the following exercise. Record yourself reading the two contrasting events:

Convey action: The police officer was fighting for his life. The suspect kept trying to rip the officer's gun out of his holster. The officer struggled to get away and keep his gun away from the suspect. The fight lasted for about a minute until other officers arrived on scene, overpowered the suspect, and took him into custody.

Convey sorrow: It was 12:30 a.m. The officers slowly approached the front porch. Like all death notifications, this one wouldn't be easy. One officer knocked on the door while the other stood a few feet back. The mother stood in silence as the officer told her, "Ma'am, I'm sorry to inform you, but your daughter was killed in a motor vehicle crash," She fell to her knees and cried.

Your tone and pace should have appropriately changed when reading each scenario. If not, then you're a monotone speaker and that needs to change. Your tone and pace should have changed to convey the action scene and the sorrowful one. This is the same idea or concept you need to apply when answering your oral interview questions. Work on adjusting your tone to convey the appropriate interest, confidence, motivation and sense of excitement.

Another way to improve your oral communications skills is through self-assessment. One insightful way to help determine how others perceive or hear you is to record yourself with a digital audio or video recorder. Ask yourself some of the sample interview questions provided in this book and answer them aloud. If you don't have a recording device available, you can also practice talking in front of a mirror. Analyze your tone, body language, and vocabulary. What do you sound like? How do you look when you communicate? In what ways can you improve? A primary benefit of using a recording device is that you can seek feedback from others. You might also find an instructor, criminal justice professional, friends, or family members who are willing to conduct a mock oral interview with you. Ask them for honest feedback and recommendations.

Use a three-step "road map" to help compose complete and professional answers during the oral interview:

- Professional-Occupational experiences
- Educational experiences
- Personal experiences

Each of these components or perspectives, in whole or in part, can be applied to most of the oral interview questions.

Professional-Occupational Experiences – when answering a question, share examples of how your *professional or occupational* experiences have helped prepare you for the position. For example, consider the following oral interview question: *"Why are you considering a career in law enforcement (or corrections)?"* In response, be prepared to share with the evaluators examples of professional or occupational experiences that have inspired or motivated you to enter the field. Many candidates do not have prior police or correctional officer experience, but there are related skills, knowledge, and experiences that are obtained in other professions, occupations, or jobs that can be directly applied to police and correctional officer positions. You must be able to come up with a reply that is consistent with this approach and related to *your* experiences. Here is an example of a successful answer from a police officer candidate who worked in the retail industry and volunteered as an auxiliary officer before entering police work.

> *"Upon graduation from high school, I was unsure what career I wanted to pursue. I was fortunate enough to do a ride-a-long at the sheriff's department and saw how the deputy interacted with the public to solve problems and fairly enforce the law. At the same time, I was working at a local bowling alley and engaged in customer service. I often had the opportunity to use my communications skills to solve customer complaints, answer telephones, and make reservations. I enjoy interacting with people, solving problems, and doing something more meaningful for the community. I like being out and active versus sitting at a desk. I then applied for and was accepted into the auxiliary police force where I participated in additional ride-a-longs (over 100 hours of experience), traffic control, security patrols, special community events (e.g., McGruff the Crime Dog, DARE, and child safe fingerprinting events). All of these combined experiences helped me confirm that my personality and communications skills would lend well towards a career in law enforcement. "*

Educational Experiences – Next, in response to the same question, be prepared to include *educational* examples that have inspired or motivated you to enter the field. Consider expanding on some topics you studied in college, such as criminal law, community policing, or corrections science. Your reply will not only allow you to tell the evaluators why you want to enter the field, but how your educational experiences are related to the real world. A sample answer from an Associate Degree criminal justice student is below.

"In order to pursue my career, I enrolled in the criminal justice program in the community college where I obtained my associate degree and graduated with honors. I took all the required courses, such as criminal law, constitutional law, criminal investigation, community policing, and professional communications. I learned how to apply the academic concepts to the real world. For example, in our community policing class I was involved in a field project where we applied the SARA model to ongoing problems downtown. I was able to see firsthand how the SARA model can be applied to solve problems in the real world."

Personal Experiences – Finally, include a *personal* example related to why you're inspired or motivated to enter the field. For example, most candidates are personally motivated to make a difference, help people, want to do something more meaningful in life, or want to seek personal justice because they are motivated by another person's tragedy. It's easy for a candidate to say these things, but the better candidate supports his/her answer with practical examples to support them. Consider the following example of a candidate who was primarily motivated by personal justice.

"I initially went to school for business, but I didn't find myself personally satisfied and wasn't very motivated to succeed. Two years ago, while still in college, a good friend of mine was killed by a drunk driver. I was very close to her and her family. I saw the emotional trauma that the death of their daughter caused them. I then saw how difficult it was for the family to sit through a jury trial. Thankfully, the police did a very good job with the case and the drunk driver was found guilty. Although the guilty verdict didn't bring my friend back, at least justice was served. I want to be a police officer to do what I can to prevent drunk driving deaths and by doing complete and thorough investigations I can help ensure that justice is fairly and properly carried out in court."

Take a moment to restate the question: *"Why are you considering a career in law enforcement (or corrections?"* Then read aloud the entire answer, from all three perspectives above. It should take you approximately two and a half minutes to answer the question. Don't forget that you're reading the answer in a stress-free environment. In an actual interview, it's likely that an answer with this much content would take about three minutes to share with the oral interview board evaluators.

Below are two common screening interview questions where the "road map" may be applied. Think about how you would answer each of these questions from a professional/occupational, personal and academic perspective. Document your "ideal answers" to both of these questions, read them aloud and evaluate your response with the guidelines given here.

- Why do you want to be a police officer for the city of Any City? Or, why do you want to be a correctional officer for Any Facility?
- What have you done to prepare yourself for the position of police officer or correctional officer?

Even if you're asked an interview question where all three aspects of the "road map" do not apply, it's likely that you can answer the question with some parts of it in mind. For example, you may be asked,

"What would you consider to be your greatest strength?" The trait that you identify (e.g., trustworthy, dependable, honest) could be highlighted from your occupational or personal experience rather than your educational experience. Approaching all interview questions with the "road map" in mind will help you meaningfully demonstrate how you're qualified for the position while taking advantage of the allotted time.

The Value of Practical Examples

Practical examples that support your oral interview answers are valuable. For example, it's relatively easy for candidates to state in general terms why they're qualified for a position. However, candidates who do well in oral interviews provide practical examples and supporting information that demonstrates why they are qualified for the position. Consider the two sample responses below to the question, "How have you prepared yourself for the position of correctional officer?"

> *"I attended a community college for two years and obtained an associate degree in corrections science. I took courses in correctional management, corrections science, and a psychology course."*

> *"I attended a community college for two years, obtained an associate degree, and graduated with honors. Some of the courses that I took included correctional science, correctional management, criminal law, and professional communications. I also had the opportunity to participate in a 40-hour internship at the county correctional facility. During the internship I had the opportunity to observe correctional officers at work and interacting with the inmates. I saw many examples that demonstrated the importance of using professional communications to deescalate situations with inmates and build relationships with them **(Academic Experience)**. While in school, I also volunteered my time at the local juvenile detention center where I created and participated in a fitness and weightlifting program for male inmates. My interactions with them helped improve my level of empathy with the offenders and build relationships with them that helped foster a cooperative environment in the institution **(Personal Experience)**. Lastly, I worked part-time as a server in a restaurant, which helped me improve my professional communications skills, especially when customers would complain about food quality. More than once, I had to use verbal deflectors, especially with intoxicated patrons that would blame me for the food quality **(Occupational Experience)**."*

Note the difference between the two responses. The first one is vague and doesn't tell the evaluators much about the candidate. *Anyone* can say that he/she went to school to become a correctional officer. This answer is short and doesn't fill the allotted time. The second response provided a complete outline and continued by explaining how the candidate's education and knowledge applies to the real world. The second response further provided the panel with personal and occupational experiences that have helped prepare the candidate for the position of correctional officer.

Prior to any criminal justice oral interview, do your "homework." Become familiar with the agency where you're applying:

- If you're applying for a police officer position, you should know the size of the department, opportunities for advancement, the rank structure, the crime rate, rate of pay and the minimum requirements needed for hire.
- For a correctional officer position, you should be familiar with the size of the institution, the types of inmates housed, opportunities for advancement, the rate of pay, and the minimum requirements for hire.

You can often obtain this information from the job announcement, their agency or municipal websites, FBI uniform crime reports, or through basic Internet searches. Candidates who are able to provide or comment on this type of information during an interview typically convey greater motivation and preparation.

Lastly, you may also be asked a scenario-based question during the oral interview. This type of question allows evaluators to help determine how a candidate prioritizes information, applies academic principles to the real world, and provides a glimpse into their ethical beliefs and standards. Whenever answering a scenario-based question, consider your response from an **ethical, legal, and policy and procedure perspective.** Most scenario- based questions will often have an ethical, legal, or policy and procedure dilemma that needs to be addressed. Consider the following scenario-based question and ideal answer:

Scenario: You and your field training officer (FTO) are dispatched to assist another officer who is out with a homeless person in a park. Upon arrival, you see the homeless person on the ground and the officer kicking him and yelling, *"Get the hell out of my park."* Your FTO turns to you and says, *"You didn't see anything, understand?"* How would you handle that situation?

> **Ideal Answer:** *"I would first intervene and perform an officer override. I would put myself in between the officer and the homeless person and do my best to stop the apparent unnecessary force. I would then check on the homeless person to see if they had any injuries that needed medical attention. If necessary, I would request that a rescue squad respond. Presuming that a rescue squad was requested, I would continue to monitor the homeless person until he was turned over to the EMS personnel. I would also check with the officer and debrief him. I would ask the officer if he was okay and about any facts or circumstances that may have precipitated the event. Consistent with the idea of Adopted Omission, if I just stood around and didn't do anything regarding this apparent unnecessary use of force, I would be just as guilty as the officer using the force. Once the scene is stabilized and the homeless person has received appropriate care, then appropriate follow through considerations must be take place. Consistent with agency policy and procedure, I would complete the necessary report narrative regarding my observations and performance at the scene and turn it in."*

Notice that in the ideal answer the candidate addressed the ethical, legal, and policy and procedure aspects of the scenario. The candidate also explained and demonstrated knowledge of the legal concept of *adopted omission*: if a (police or correctional) officer sees something that is unethical, illegal, or a violation of policy and procedure and does nothing about it, he or she is just as guilty as the officer engaging in the behavior.

A member of the panel will advise you when the interview is over and again ask if there are any questions. Again, if you have any questions about the interview or the rest of the hiring process, ask them now. If you indicate that you don't have any questions, they will thank you for participating. Prior to leaving, it's acceptable to thank the panel with an appropriate parting comment such as *"Thank you for providing me with this opportunity"* or *"Thank you, I look forward to participating in the rest of the hiring process."*

Oral Interview Evaluation

The results of the oral interview process are often evaluated with a numerical point system. A one- to five-point system is common with 1 being "poor" and 5 being "superior." There are also various categories of evaluation, including preparation and motivation, knowledge, diversity, communication skills and appearance. The evaluators will typically complete the evaluation form immediately after you leave. See Figure 6 for an example of an evaluation form.

Internet Extra

A practical example of how to implement the oral board interview "Road Map" advocated in this chapter can be viewed at the following Internet hyperlink: https://www.youtube.com/watch?v=uqBHKbABOTg. If the link does not work conduct a "YouTube" ™ search for, *Preparing for the Criminal Justice Oral Board Interview.*

Figure 6 - Sample Oral Board Interview Evaluation Form – Police Officer Candidate

This evaluation form is not an endorsement or recommendation, but merely contains example criteria and categories of evaluation that may be used to determine if a candidate passes the oral board interview and successfully moves on to the next step of the hiring process.

Candidate Name: **Evaluator(s):**

Evaluation should be based on information presented during the interview, not based on assumptions or what the evaluator feels the candidate might have meant. Consider the information presented regarding knowledge, skills, and abilities within each dimension as explained below. Questions are specific to each dimension, however information provided in other questions may apply to multiple dimensions. Scores will be based on the following scale. Please provide helpful and honest feedback.

1	2	3	4	5
Unacceptable	Below average, can be satisfactory, needs some improvement	Average, satisfactory knowledge, skills and abilities	Above average knowledge, skills and abilities	Excellent, superior knowledge, skills and abilities

Dimension	Score
Preparation for Law Enforcement: Can clearly demonstrate commitment to preparation relative to law enforcement including education and related work experience. Candidate has shown initiative in distinguishing himself/herself as a well-prepared candidate. Candidate has demonstrated this through intelligence, work ethic, education and career orientation. Evaluator Comments:	
Motivation: Can clearly and concisely explain impetus for wanting to become a Patrol Officer, as well as the aspects of law enforcement that motivate him/her the most; fully understands the duties, responsibilities and demands of the work. Candidate's response indicates that he/she is familiar with the police operations. Impetus is realistic and clearly thought through. Evaluator Comments:	
Ethics: Candidate clearly acknowledges the importance of ethical behavior by police department personnel and that unethical behavior is unacceptable and cannot be tolerated. Response demonstrates that the candidate possesses integrity. Candidate understands the importance of informing a superior officer of any inappropriate behavior he/she is made aware of or seeking direction from a superior when there is a question that could impact the integrity of the employee and/or the police department. Candidate's response indicates the potential criminal or civil liability and policy violations if proper protocol is not followed. **(Based on a scenario)** Evaluator Comments:	
Diversity/Human Relations: Ability to recognize legitimate differences between cultures, races, age groups, religions, etc. Acknowledges that diversity within the community and the police department can greatly impact law enforcement. Recognizes that communication, language barriers, religious practices, cultural issues, dealing with the disabled or elderly are diversity issues that impact law enforcement. Projects authority, respect, empathy, sensitivity, and openness where appropriate. Understands and appreciates differences, avoiding inappropriate slurs/epithets. Recognizes and shows respect for diversity. Utilizes resources available to gain a greater understanding of diversity and to more effectively work with people of diverse backgrounds. Evaluator Comments:	
Overall Communication Skills/Presentation: Speaks clearly and concisely, understandable to almost anyone he/she is likely to contact on the job. Speaks directly to a question or issue without confusion, disorganization or rambling. Discusses topics thoroughly, but without losing sight of situational needs to avoid overly lengthy explanations or comments. Sensitive and responsive to differing communication requirements with whom he/she speaks. Technical qualities of oral expression (volume, rate, vocabulary) do not distract from basic clarity of communication (regional dialects and accents are irrelevant and are not regarded as "technical qualities"). Candidate listened closely and responded accordingly. Candidate is reasonably comfortable and confident with interview stress. Evaluator Comments:	
Appearance, Manner and Bearing: Will his or her appearance (today), manner, or bearing help or hinder him/her in this job. Will he/she be able to develop effective contacts with the public or other law enforcement officers? Does he/she appear to have the presence necessary to establish respect and confidence? Are they appropriately dressed for the interview environment? Does their presence or way they convey themselves (e.g., posture) convey confidence and professional presence? Evaluator Comments:	
Total Score or Calculated Average	

Each evaluation category or dimension from the oral board evaluation form is listed in the following chart with recommendations regarding best practices and preparation for performing well within each dimension.

Criteria/Dimension	Recommended Responses
Preparation	Highlight your education, related work experience, volunteer opportunities, and provide examples of how they relate to your desired position.
Motivation	Provide a response that demonstrates you understand the roles of a police or correctional officer. Share with them a realistic motivation for wanting to become a police or correctional officer. Study the agency that you want to work for and tell them what you know about it (e.g., size of the agency, opportunities, nature of crime, size of the correctional facility, number of beds, programs).
Ethics	Provide a response that addresses any ethical, moral, legal, or police and procedure dilemmas that are present. Be sure to include follow through and notification of inappropriate behavior to a supervisor. Your response should convey that you believe in individual responsibility and accountability. After all, police and correctional officers are supposed to be "above and beyond" in this dimension.
Diversity / Human Relations	Highlight examples in your life that demonstrate you can work with diverse populations. Do you speak a foreign language? Have you worked with diverse populations? Did you grow up in a diverse area? Were you in the military and served overseas? Highlight that diversity is more than just race, but also disability, socioeconomic status, religious beliefs, and sexual orientation. Essentially, diversity exists any time there is a different viewpoint because our beliefs, values, and perspectives are all influenced or shaped by diversity.
Communications Skills	Prepare for you interview and practice your ideal answers. Preparation will allow you to speak more clearly and confidently. Practice removing "ah" and "um" when speaking. Keep your posture upright and forward. Use your hands to emphasize points and address the entire board with appropriate eye contact when speaking.
Appearance	Dress the part! Men, wear a suit, tie, and matching shoes. Women, wear a blouse, slacks, and matching shoes. It is recommended that you select dark or conservative colors, such as black, navy blue, or shades of gray.

The criteria help evaluators determine how well you performed during the oral interview. If you apply the recommended "road map" for answering oral interview questions, the responses should allow you to address much of the criteria within each evaluation category.

The oral interview process is demanding and rarely does anyone "ace" the first one. To help yourself improve, upon completion of an oral interview, after you've left the interview environment, write down the questions you were asked, your responses, and the likely "ideal" response they were seeking. As you participate in other oral interviews, you'll find many of the questions are similar and your responses will improve. Like many aspects of life, improving your oral interview performance takes time and practice. The more you prepare and practice for an oral interview, the more successful you'll be. If you successfully pass the full panel oral board interview, you'll then move onto the next step, the physical agility test.

No resource can provide the answers to *all* potential oral interview questions that you might be asked. The answers must come from you! However, applying the principles here will allow you to formulate complete and meaningful answers. Take the time to compose ideal answers to each of the potential interview questions provided in this chapter. Restate the questions aloud and practice your ideal answers. Practice in front of a mirror, record yourself, or participate in a mock oral interview board. You must be honest in your self-assessment and evaluation of the answers that you come up with, but also in the nature of your communications skills. Improving your communications skills takes great effort, time and patience.

Step 4 – Physical Agility

If you successfully complete the screening interview or otherwise move forward in the application process, the next step is typically a physical agility test. This test (and all other tests discussed thus far) must be considered "valid" and "reliable." A test is deemed "valid" when it measures job-related abilities. A test is deemed "reliable" when the results are consistent and stable over time under similar circumstances. Therefore, the type of physical agility or ability test administered must be directly related to the position and administered to all candidates under similar conditions.

Your preparation for the police officer or correctional officer physical fitness test must begin well before test day. It's also critical to your long-term success to make exercise a lifelong habit, which will help sustain you throughout your career and help prevent injuries. The benchmarks for the physical agility test are commonly provided to you at the time of the test.

A police or correctional agency can create its own physical agility test or use a standardized one that has been deemed valid and reliable. For example, the Utah Department of Public Safety uses a standardized physical fitness test battery that consists of a vertical jump measurement, maximum sit-ups, maximum push-ups, 300 meter run, and a 1.5 mile run. The "pass" or "fail" standards for each test are often dependent upon age and gender. Go to http://publicsafety.utah.gov/post/pdf/PT.pdf for an example of "Superior," "Excellent," and "Good" performance for each test battery.

Other agencies use a physical agility test to measure a candidate's level of overall fitness. A common physical agility test used by police departments across the country is an obstacle course that simulates the physical hazards and demands that police officers encounter in the field. For example, the City of Green Bay (WI) Police Department administers an obstacle course that simulates a foot pursuit through a city environment. The obstacle course requires all candidates to successfully perform the following while wearing a ballistic vest:

- While seated in a patrol car with the seat belt fastened and hands on the steering wheel, the candidate will receive a verbal description of a subject. With this description, the candidate must visually identify one of four subjects while running the course. Upon being given an instruction to begin, the candidate will unbuckle the seatbelt and exit the car.
- Move through a simulated culvert approximately 42" high and 15' in length.
- Climb through a simulated window approximately 38" off the ground.
- Quickly climb and descend two flights of stairs, touching each stair tread going up and down.
- Climb over a four-foot high and a five-foot high barrier.
- Run an obstacle course of approximately 450 feet inclusive of all obstacles, including a serpentine course and running an indoor track.
- Move a 150-pound dummy a distance of 35 feet by carrying, pulling or dragging it.
- Operate the slide mechanism on an empty, unloaded semi-automatic pistol five times in rapid succession. The candidate will pull the trigger five times in rapid succession with each hand.

Correctional agencies may also offer a physical agility test other than a standardized one. For example, New York Department of Civil Service requires all correctional officer candidates to successfully pass the following physical agility test battery:

- **Stair Climb Test** – The candidate must go up and down a flight of stairs one time.
- **Ladder Ascent** – The candidate safely climbs to a height of 12 feet, the ladder encased by a standard industrial safety cage with an interior dimension of approximately 30 inches, until the designated rung is touched. The candidate then descends to the floor in a safe manner.
- **Suspended Dummy Raise** – The candidate must lift a 120-pound hanging dummy (using a bear hug) high enough to relieve the tension on the rope (thereby taking pressure off the neck) and hold for 5 seconds.
- **Body Transport Test** – The candidate must pull a 160-pound dummy on a blanket for 30 feet.
- **Obstacle Vault** – The candidate must be able to get over a three-foot high obstacle in a safe manner (hurdling or diving not permitted).
- **Door Lock and Unlock** – The candidate must properly unlock a standard use security cell door, using the assigned key, go through the door and relock the same door.
- **Load and Unload** – The candidate must properly load and unload a designated firearm in a safe manner.
- **Three-Minute Step Test** –The candidate will lift one foot at a time while stepping on and off a 12 inch high bench. The candidate must keep pace with a metronome set at 96 beats per minute. Immediately after the three minutes, with the candidate sitting, a 60-second heart rate count is taken starting five seconds after the completion of stepping.

Source: http://www.cs.state.ny.us/ehs/agilities/ag_1_correction_officer_description.pdf

If you pass the physical agility test, you will be ranked based upon all of the test results thus far, including your scores on the written test, screening interview and the physical agility portion.

Step 5 – Ranking of Successful Candidates

Based upon your performance in the first five steps, you will be ranked numerically from number one to the end of the list. The top-ranked candidate has performed best thus far. You will typically be notified via mail or email regarding whether or not you've been successfully ranked to the eligibility list or if you're no longer being considered for employment.

If you won't be continuing in the process, it's normal to wonder why you were eliminated and desire feedback on how to improve. Unfortunately, an employment law "best practice" is not to share reasons for elimination. This prevents the municipality from exposure to any potential legal action. If you contact a human resources division to find out why you were eliminated, the answer is often, *"I'm sorry, I can't provide you with that information."* The best way to determine why you were eliminated from the process is to note immediately upon completion of the interview the questions asked, your responses, and the ideal response that the agency was likely seeking. Through honest assessment and self-reflection, you'll find areas for improvement. If you didn't meet the minimum physical requirements, make it a goal to improve through regular exercise and healthy eating habits.

If your ranking means you'll be continuing in the employment process, congratulations! However, the remaining steps of the criminal justice hiring process are even more intense as you enter the background investigation phase. A background investigation questionnaire may be included with the correspondence notifying you of your ranking or other notification that you're moving on in the process. The most important thing to remember regarding the background investigation is to be *honest*.

Step 6 - Background Investigation

The background investigation is a thorough examination of your occupational, educational, and personal life. Unfortunately, many candidates do not pass the background investigation. Before the background investigation begins, the agency will request the candidate sign a release of information form. Copies of this form are sent to various entities, individuals, businesses and institutions the investigators may visit or inquire with when conducting your background investigation. The form will also advise you of the extent of the background investigation, including inquiries into credit scores or examination of social media sites. See Figure 7 for a sample release of information form.

Figure 7 - Sample Background Investigation Release Form

The document will be used by the Human Resources Department for the sole purpose of conducting necessary background checks on potential candidates for positions with the police/correctional agency. Retention of this personal data will be kept separate from your application and will remain in confidential files of the Human Resources Department.

The undersigned [police/correctional candidate] hereby authorizes inspection, review, copying and full disclosure of all records concerning myself to any representative of the [police/correctional agency], whether said records are of a public, private, or confidential nature.

The intent of this authorization is to give my full consent for full and complete disclosure of information and records from any source, including, but not limited to the following:

1. Any educational institution.

2. Any business, public utility, financial or credit institution to obtain financial statements, records of loans, credit reports or ratings, or other records.

3. Military records, including U.S. Veteran's Administration and Selective Service System.

4. Employment, past employment and pre-employment records including, but not limited to, applications, background reports, complaints or grievances filed by or against [applicant], disciplinary reports or letters, performance evaluations, supervisors' comments, wage rates, and work records.

5. Records and recollections of attorneys at law, or other counsel representing [applicant] or any other person in any case, criminal or civil, in which [applicant] presently has, or have had, an interest.

6. Any public or private social service agency.

7. Friends, relatives, or neighbors.

8. Juvenile records.

I [applicant] understand that any information obtain directly or indirectly pursuant to this release will be considered in determining my suitability for employment or in connection with continued employment.

I release any individual, institution, or organization, including its officers, employees, and related personnel, both individually and collectively, from any and all liability for damages of whatever kind relating to the disclosure of this information.

This consent shall remain in effect for one year from this date or the duration of my employment or whichever is longer. A photocopy of this authorization shall be considered as valid as the original.

Signature/Date _____   Print Name_____

Once again, the most important aspect of the background investigation is *honesty*. Agencies must know they are hiring honest and ethical candidates who reflect the agency's mission and values. Of course, they must also determine that you are not a convicted felon, which is an automatic disqualification. Agencies will also evaluate whether or not certain other convictions may eliminate you. Evidence of certain crimes, especially those referred to as "crimes against moral turpitude," will also eliminate you. A crime against moral turpitude is a legal concept that refers to conduct that is considered contrary to community standards of justice, honesty or good morals. The most common elements of crimes involving moral turpitude are fraud, larceny or theft, and the intent to harm people or property (e.g., arson, blackmail, burglary, extortion, criminal damage to property, or robbery). Criminal arrests or convictions for felony crimes or misdemeanor crimes of violence, such as domestic violence, will prohibit you from obtaining employment.

Agencies will also evaluate your driving record for convictions that may indicate immaturity or irresponsibility. Some traffic-related convictions that may disqualify you include operating after suspension or revocation, operating while intoxicated, reckless driving, or racing on a highway. Of course, you must possess a valid driver's license at the time of application.

It's not uncommon for those who want to become police or correctional officers to have some questions about how their background will affect their chances of finding employment. Positions for police and correctional officers are limited and it's not uncommon for hundreds of candidates to apply for only a few positions. Although you may not have an automatically disqualifying arrest or conviction in your background, prior arrests or police contacts could negatively affect your chances of success. For example, presume that there are five final candidates for four positions. Out of those candidates, four of them have no prior criminal arrests or convictions of any sort. However, the remaining candidate has one prior arrest and citation for simple possession of marijuana and a prior, non-criminal citation for reckless driving. Which candidate is most likely to be eliminated from the remaining five? You probably know the answer. Therefore, no matter how minor previous citations or convictions might be, they can work against you when competing with other candidates who have clean records. Naturally, people make mistakes and mature as they age. If you have some prior arrests or citations, it's imperative that you make efforts to demonstrate that you've changed. Some indications that you've become a good candidate include participating in volunteer work, surrounding yourself with good people, maintaining steady employment, and avoiding social settings or situations, such as excessive drinking or social drug use, that might make you appear irresponsible or immature.

The background investigation continues by thoroughly examining your personal, educational, financial, and occupational background. Background investigators usually interview you before they begin the background investigation. At the background investigation interview, you will present the completed background packet, which will be reviewed by the investigators. The investigators will scrutinize the packet, ask any initial questions, and reiterate the importance of honesty and completeness regarding this step of the process. If any information has changed, such as your current employer, be sure to update the investigators. This is also the best time for you to ask any questions or offer any clarifying statements. Anything withheld in the completed background investigation packet or by you during the interview will likely be considered deceitful and used to disqualify you from any further employment proceedings. Again, *honesty* is the key. Don't "forget" to document or share that a past employer fired you because you're afraid it will be used against you. It might very well be viewed negatively; however, it's worse to lie or withhold information. Consider the following real world example.

> *Amanda applied for the position of patrol officer and was told to be completely honest in the background investigation phase. Amanda withheld the name of an employer because she had been fired, five years earlier, under suspicion of employee theft. Amanda believed that her termination, because it involved an allegation of employee theft, would prevent her from getting hired as a police officer. During the background investigation, the withheld employer was discovered and interviewed. Of course, the employer revealed that Amanda had been fired for suspicion of employee theft. Amanda's withholding of information automatically disqualified her from the police officer hiring process. A year later, the same employer who had fired Amanda hired her back! Had Amanda revealed this employer in the background packet and/or during the interview with the background investigators, she would have likely passed the background check and realized her goal of becoming a police officer.*

Police and correctional agencies are not looking for perfect candidates; rather they are looking for *honest* candidates. If you cannot be honest in the background investigation stage, then how can they expect you to honestly perform your important job functions and duties with little or no supervision? See Figure 8 for a sample list of background interview questions.

Figure 8 - Sample Background Investigation Questions

1. Is there anything that you forgot or intentionally left off your application?
2. Have you listed all of your previous addresses for the past seven years?
3. Have you ever gone by a different name?
4. Are you currently on any other agencies hiring or eligibility list?
5. Are there any other jobs that you forgot to list on your application?
6. Have you ever been asked or told to leave a job?
7. Have you ever been terminated from any job?
8. Have you ever left a job without giving proper notice?
9. Have you ever been named or filed a civil lawsuit, including any job related lawsuit?
10. Have you ever filed for bankruptcy?
11. Have you ever had your wages garnished?
12. Have you ever been more than 30-days late for a credit payment?
13. Are you behind in credit payments right now?
14. Have you ever been evicted from a residence?
15. Have you ever taken anything from a place of employment?
16. Have you ever taken any money from an employer?
17. Have you ever falsified or changed your or another employees time card?
18. Have you ever left work without permission?
19. Have you ever taken anything out of a store without paying for it?
20. Have you ever purposely damaged property to get a discount or reduced price?
21. Have you ever used, sold, or possessed any illegal drugs?
22. Have you ever gone to work or school "high" or "stoned"?
23. Have you ever used your own medication to get "high"?
24. Have you ever missed work or class because of drinking?
25. Have you ever driven "intoxicated" or "impaired"?

This is not an all-inclusive list. The sample questions provided come from nearly 100 background investigation questions that could be asked.

Once you've answered all of the questions in the background packet, the investigators will then use the information as part of their investigation of your background. In addition to examining your criminal records, police contacts in all places that you have lived, and looking at your credit history, the background investigators will also interview your immediate family members, neighbors, teachers and friends. The information provided is also used to find other people not listed who might have information about you. For example, one question may have asked you to list neighbors you grew up with. The background investigators will make contact with these people, but also ask them, *"Do you know anybody else we could talk to that might have information about Jim?"* The investigators want to get as much unbiased information about you as possible. Your honesty when completing the background investigation packet and during the interview with the investigators will leave you little to be concerned about. Regrettably, many potentially well qualified and good candidates are eliminated from the process because they withheld information that was eventually discovered by the investigators.

Keep in mind that the background investigators aren't looking for a "perfect" candidate who has never made a mistake in his/her lifetime or had contact with law enforcement. Nobody is perfect. However, when encountering candidates who have had law enforcement contact, the investigators attempt to determine if they've learned from their mistakes and matured. It is problematic if a 25-year-old candidate was issued a citation for disorderly conduct at the age of 17, but then received another citation for disorderly conduct at the age of 23. This would indicate a pattern of undesirable behavior. However, it would be viewed differently if the same candidate didn't have any law enforcement contact since they were 17 and appeared to have learned and matured from the first experience. Candidates who have a pattern of poor lifestyle choices such as drug use or a poor financial history or decisions (e.g., law enforcement contact) are not likely to pass the background investigation and will be disqualified.

Many criminal justice students have asked about how a juvenile arrest may impact their ability to become a police or correctional officer. Juvenile criminal matters are considered confidential unless the offender is waived to adult court. Otherwise, juvenile arrest records will not appear in online database searches or within other publicly available resources. If the juvenile arrest was an ordinance violation, it will not appear in state criminal history databases.

However, the police incident report and associated information about the arrest will exist in local police files. Background investigators will most likely find out about the juvenile arrest when they submit records requests to all local police departments in communities where you've lived. If the juvenile arrest was a misdemeanor or felony, it may appear within the state criminal history databases and will be discovered when your name is queried.

The impact of any arrest, juvenile or adult, will vary depending upon the totality of the circumstances. Obviously, an ordinance violation citation for retail theft will have less impact than a misdemeanor arrest for criminal damage to property. Consistent with adult arrests, a juvenile felony conviction will eliminate you from the process. The goal of any juvenile justice system is to keep you out of the system and provide you with second chances. Background investigators are more likely to accept a candidate who has learned from immature mistakes and taken advantage of those second chances versus those who continued to be involved in criminal activity.

The issue of prior drug use is another frequently asked question. The most commonly used illegal drug in the U.S. is marijuana. It is not uncommon for teens or young adults to have used marijuana in their lifetime. It's also not uncommon to have consumed alcohol prior to the legal drinking age. It is unlikely that prior social use of marijuana or underage drinking will eliminate a candidate. Agencies are more concerned with chemical addictions, which may be indicative by regular uses of marijuana or alcohol. Of course, the use of more dangerous drugs, such as cocaine, heroin, or methamphetamines, which are highly addictive, will raise significant concern. Additional inquiry into a candidate's drug or alcohol use will take place during a polygraph test and/or psychological examination.

Criminal association is another aspect of the background investigation that will be examined. Although it is not illegal to be in a relationship with, related to, acquainted or friends with others who have a criminal record, it could negatively affect your ability to pass the background investigation. Consider the following real-world scenario:

> Jim had done well in the patrol officer hiring process and was now in the background investigation stage. During his meeting with the background investigators, Jim presented his completed background packet, which also included all the states he had previously lived in. Jim didn't reveal a local police contact in another state, which the background investigators discovered during their investigation. Although Jim wasn't arrested in the case (which is why he didn't feel the need to reveal it), it was discovered that he was "friends" with and present when some criminal gang members were arrested for unlawfully being in possession of firearms. Jim was eliminated from the background investigation for "failure to disclose," but the investigators also cited his "criminal gang affiliation" as another factor.

The closer you are to the criminal association, the more cause for concern. For example, a criminal justice student once asked, *"My husband is a convicted felon. Will this prevent me from becoming a police officer?"* Because there is a very close, emotional, and personal association to a convicted felon, the cause for concern is greater than if you were loosely affiliated with a convicted felon a few years prior, with whom you're no longer in contact.

Why is there such a concern about your personal relationships and acquaintances? As a police or correctional officer, you will be responsible for ensuring that policies, procedures, and laws related to privacy and confidentiality are followed. Obviously, background investigators become concerned about any criminal associations that may seek out investigative or confidential information, including personal information about officers. Unfortunately, there have been instances across the United States where police or correctional officers are terminated for violating privacy and confidentiality laws or policies. For example, correctional officers have been terminated for becoming romantically involved with inmates and police officers have been terminated for revealing investigative information to "tip off" a friend to help avoid arrest or detection.

Be careful of the company you keep because it will reflect upon your character. Begin to surround yourself with good, moral, and ethical people today.

The "Social Media" Check

You should assume that background investigators will look at your social media web pages for any illegal or questionable content. Therefore, you should anticipate that what you post on your social media web sites today will be viewed by a police background investigator in the future. You don't have any First Amendment protections for information that you post freely on the Internet. Presume that others are going to see your posts and the potential interpretation of them. Many candidates don't consider their prior posts, photos, and videos and how it may affect the background investigation. For example, photos of you participating in underage drinking, drug use, or negative personal affiliations (e.g., with known criminals or gang members), along with vulgar and inappropriate posts will negatively affect you and could be used as a disqualifying factor. As the background investigation begins, you might consider deleting perceived or actual inappropriate materials; however, just because they are deleted doesn't mean they're gone. If you desire to seek employment in the criminal justice field, consider the impact of your social media pages *today*.

Agencies that conduct the social media check will typically have you log into your social media site(s) and then have you leave the room while the investigators examine the content. The background investigators will look at all posts, images, videos, and other content associated with your social media account. Agencies are cautious not to eliminate you solely on a post that might be ethically or morally questionable. Agencies are aware that it might be a violation of state law or First Amendment rights to use a post to eliminate a candidate, unless the post is clearly unlawful. For example, an image of you using illegal drugs can be used against you because it's unlawful behavior. Even though other posts may not be illegal, if they are politically divisive, considered insensitive, or reflect negatively against one race or another, they will reflect negatively upon you.

The Credit Check
Agencies will also conduct a thorough examination of your credit history. Although a credit score can provide a snap shot, the examination of your credit history is more extensive. Credit scores can range from 300 to 850 with the related rank:

- Above 750: excellent credit
- 700-750: very good credit
- 650-700: good credit
- 600-650: bad credit
- Below 600: very bad credit

In addition to the credit score, the background investigators will also examine the number of credit cards and debt, payment history (on time or late), and whether or not any of your accounts are or have been in collections. Although the credit history is just one piece of the background investigation, it's a very important part, and poor credit and credit history often reveals a poor candidate.

Another check that is sometimes done in conjunction with the credit check is a query with the IRS that reveals a history of income and employers, including any W-9 forms that were filed for part-time, temporary, or contract work. The results are often used to verify that you have listed all employers on the background and application packet. As mentioned earlier, sometimes candidates choose to omit employers who have terminated them out of fear that it would affect their employment prospects. Even if you've been terminated from previous positions, once again, it's best to be *honest* and explain. Failure to disclose a complete employment history may cause you to fail the background investigation.

In summary, *honesty* is the key to passing the criminal justice background investigation. Full disclosure is the expectation. Don't eliminate yourself by withholding information that you perceive as detrimental. If you have some past police contacts or minor arrests, begin demonstrating today that you have changed. Police and correctional officer candidates can demonstrate that they have changed by making healthy lifestyle choices, surrounding themselves with great people, participating in volunteer work, maintaining steady employment and networking with successful criminal justice professionals.

If you successfully complete the background investigation, you will then receive a conditional offer of employment. The conditional offer is a formal offer of employment that is contingent upon successfully completing a polygraph exam, psychological exam, and medical screening. These three final examinations are discussed next.

Step 7 - Conditional Offer of Employment

If you successfully complete the background investigation you will likely receive a conditional offer of employment. The conditional offer is contingent upon successful completion of the polygraph, psychological screening, and medical screening. The dates for the remaining steps in the process will be determined by the employing agency and you will be notified by post or via email.

Polygraph Examination

Where allowed by law and used by the hiring agency, candidates will undergo a polygraph examination. You should explore the laws in your state regarding the use of polygraph examinations for criminal justice pre-employment. Your state may not permit a polygraph examination for private sector or non-criminal justice positions. However, it is likely that there are exceptions in the laws permitting the use of a polygraph for criminal justice-related positions.

This step serves as a check and balance on the results of the background investigation. The background investigators may have obtained some additional information that you didn't provide and may ask you about it during the examination. The examination is also yet another check on honesty and truthfulness. Again, if you continue to be completely honest and truthful throughout the process, you have little to worry about. An examination of the polygraph machine and explanation regarding how it works will help to better prepare you for this stage of the hiring process.

A polygraph is not a "lie detector"; rather, it measures changes in physiological arousal in response to a set of questions. Recorded physiological changes in response to certain questions are deemed to be indicators of deceit that deserve further inquiry. There are no standard physiological responses unique to deception. Instead, the polygraph examiners document the physiological changes in response to a controlled set of questions. There are normally three different types of physiological responses that are measured: the rate and depth of respiration, cardiovascular activity, and skin perspiration.

Most criminal justice employment polygraph examinations last anywhere from 30 to 60 minutes. Upon entering the room, the examiner should explain how the test will proceed. Because this is a condition of your potential employment, refusing to participate in the test is grounds to remove you from the hiring process. The examiner will then attach the three physiological measuring devices: a blood pressure cuff, a strap around your chest or abdomen to measure depth and rate of breathing, and an electro-dermal response device to your finger to measure perspiration. The questioning will then begin.

The initial questions are typically used to establish a physiological baseline regarding what your physiological responses are when you are truthful. Simple questions that you have no reason to lie about are often asked, such as, *"Where did you go to high school?"* or *"What was the name of your high school mascot?"* Once this baseline is established, the pre-employment questions will be asked next.

The pre-employment questions should be standard for every candidate participating in the polygraph examination. A relevant pre-employment question might be, *"Is there anything in your background of interest that you have not revealed to us?"* During the questioning, there are often some irrelevant questions asked, such as, *"What day is it today?"* The irrelevant questions establish the normal or baseline level of arousal, which is later compared to the physiological responses to relevant questions. Some of the more common relevant pre-employment questions are:

- Did you tell the complete truth on your application?
- Have you deliberately withheld any information in your background investigation packet that you filled out?
- Have you deliberately lied when answering any of these questions?
- In the past five years, have you stolen anything from a previous employer?
- In the last ten years, have you participated in or committed any serious crimes?

A typical pre-employment polygraph examination may involve those five relevant questions listed above. However, after each relevant question, an irrelevant question may be asked to continually measure the physiological response to questions that you have no motive to lie about. Once all questions are asked, the polygraph examiner may analyze and mark the polygraph report to identify the beginning and end of the series of questions. It's then common to repeat the same series of questions two or three times to get the most accurate physiological results.

Upon conclusion, the polygraph examiner will evaluate the results and may ask some clarifying questions. Typically, the examiner will not tell you how you performed. Instead, he/she will advise that the results will be sent to your potential employer and they will follow up with you later regarding the results. The polygraph examiner will draft a report regarding his/her conclusions regarding whether or not you were truthful or displayed indicators of deceit during the test. The polygraph examiners report will become part of the overall background investigation and included in the decision to hire or not hire you.

Psychological Screening
Upon successful completion of the polygraph, you'll then move on to the psychological screening. Due to the unique nature of the demands upon police and correctional officers, the constant contact with people in potentially volatile situations, and the authority to use force, along with increased risk of suicide and substance abuse, it is necessary that candidates for these positions be psychologically healthy and fit for the job.

The reason for the psychological screening is to establish that you're emotionally stable, and are psychologically fit to perform as a police or correctional officer. The screening also confirms you're not suffering from mental illness or prone to substance abuse or other addictions such as gambling. Psychological screening does not determine your sanity or lack thereof and failing the exam does not mean you're crazy (Roufa, n.d.).

There is not one standard police psychological screening test or tool used across the country. However, some are used more often than others. The more common criminal justice psychological screening tests include the following:

- Minnesota Multi-Phasic Personality Inventory – II (MMPI- II)
- Inwald Personality Inventory (IPI)
- California Psychological Inventory (CPI)
- Personality Assessment Inventory (PAI)
- NEO Personality Inventory
- Wonderlic Personality Test

Internet keyword searches will reveal additional information regarding each of these psychological screening tests, including sample tests that will give you an idea regarding your psychological profile. Currently the MMPI – II is the most commonly used psychological test followed by the IPI (Dantzker, 2011). There is no way to accurately predict what psychological screening tool will be used by agencies where you apply. There is also no way to prepare or study for the psychological screening. The best recommendation is to ensure that you're completely honest during the assessment. There are built-in measures to identify lying and inconsistency during the assessment, which can be a red flag used against recommending you.

Upon completion of the psychological test, the psychologist or psychiatrist will evaluate the results and then schedule an interview with you. If you are among a small number of candidates, you may have the follow-up interview the same day. Where candidate pools are larger, the follow-up interview may take place weeks later. The agency should make you aware of these timelines during this stage of the process.

The results of the psychological exam do not indicate whether or not you "pass" or "fail" it. Rather, the results of the test and the follow-up interview allow the psychologist or psychiatrist to make a recommendation regarding whether or not you're fit for police or correctional work. Depending on the tool or test used, there are several dimensions that are part of the overall evaluation. These include but are not limited to the following:

- Alcohol and drug use
- Honesty and integrity
- Trouble with law and society
- Antisocial attitudes
- Driving violations
- Job difficulties

- Anxiety
- Obsessive personality
- Depression
- Family conflicts
- Judgment
- Conflict resolution skills
- Absence of bias
- Attitudes toward supervision
- Reasonable courage
- Stress tolerance

Upon conclusion of the assessment, the clinical psychologist or psychiatrist will not simply say that you passed. Instead, according to Miller (2007), you may be assessed as having one of three common levels of risk: low, medium or high.

The psychologist or psychiatrist may "Recommend" or "Not Recommend" you based upon the assessment results. However, it is ultimately up to the agency whether or not to keep you in the hiring process. Obviously, it is unlikely that a law enforcement or correctional agency would hire a candidate who is considered "high risk." Low-risk candidates are what agencies ideally seek; medium-risk candidates may be given further consideration on a case-by-case basis.

The psychological screening of police and correctional officer candidates is necessary to help identify the best qualified. It is essential that you are honest during the assessment even if you don't feel comfortable talking about some of the subjects, such as questions related to sexual activity or alcohol and drug use. Remember, police and correctional agencies are not looking for perfect candidates, but are looking for *honest* ones.

Medical screening

The medical screening is often the last step in the extensive criminal justice hiring process. The primary reason for this step is to determine if you are physically healthy enough and able to perform all of the *essential physical duties* of a police or correctional officer. Some of those duties include making forcible arrests; loading, firing, or unloading a firearm; running after a fleeing person; lifting or dragging people; directing traffic for long periods of time; performing searches of people or escorting them from one location to another; and wearing a gas mask in situations where chemical munitions are used.

There are some medical conditions that may eliminate you from employment, such as a history of seizures, breathing problems that prohibit anaerobic exercise, or cancer. There are also some medical conditions you might think eliminate you when they actually don't, such as well-controlled diabetes or asthma. It's impossible to conclude which medical conditions might eliminate you for one agency, but could be considered acceptable to another. For example, some agencies may refuse to hire a candidate with asthma or diabetes, while others still would. If you have a serious medical condition, such as a recent seizure or a severe heart or lung condition, it might preclude you from becoming a police or correctional officer. If you think you might have a serious health condition, you should consult your physician to help determine the extent to which it might affect your ability to perform the essential duties of police or correctional officers.   As long as you can perform all of the essential physical duties of a police or correctional officer, you should have no problem passing the medical examination.

Your physical examination will begin with a questionnaire that asks you to self-report on your health, including any medical conditions that you might have. Like all other steps in the hiring process, it's essential that you are *honest*. Failing to disclose a known medical condition can be cause to remove you from the hiring process. The physician will review the questionnaire with you, ask any clarifying questions, and then begin the exam. Your physical examination will include an analysis of your vital signs, vision, hearing, breathing and a complete blood panel. Additional tests may be recommended based upon what you self-reported or what was discovered during the examination. For example, you could be required to participate in cardiac stress testing or additional pulmonary function tests to determine your ability to wear a respirator (gas mask).

In addition to the physical examination, a drug screen or analysis test will be conducted. At some time in the process, you will have been asked questions related to past drug use. Typically, the presence of any illicit drugs, without a documented and valid medical reason, will be considered an automatic disqualification and prevent employment. The drugs most often tested for are amphetamines, cannabis or cannabinoids, opiates, cocaine, or phencyclidine (PCP).

Successfully completing the polygraph, psychological, and medical examinations are the last steps in the thorough police officer or correctional officer hiring processes. Now is the time to begin or maintain healthy physical and psychological lifestyle choices that will enhance your ability to successfully pass these final steps and find yourself one step closer to putting the uniform on for the first time.

Step 8 - Official Job Offer with Starting Date

Congratulations! If you've received an official job offer with a starting date, you have persevered and successfully completed the extensive criminal justice hiring process. Although this marks the end of one process, it is the beginning of another. Upon hire, police and correctional officers must complete an academy and/or extensive on-the-job training. Larger agencies will have their own police and correctional academies. Smaller agencies will often utilize an academy administered by a regional community or technical college. In some states (e.g., Wisconsin), candidates have already completed the courses and training that allow them to be "certified" police or correctional officers as part of their education and can enter the training phase upon hire.

All police and correctional agencies require new officers to complete a probationary period. The probationary period can last anywhere from six to 18 months. During this probationary period, you can be released "without cause" and are considered an "at will" employee. However, being released without cause is unlikely and uncommon. Officers that are released or terminated during their probationary period have often demonstrated that they are unfit for the position or cannot carry out the necessary duties. Agencies have invested far too much money, time, resources, and energy to simply release you without cause. Furthermore, agencies are always vigilant against lawsuits and do not want to create a situation where they may be successfully sued for unlawful termination.

The training phase in both police and correctional agencies is referred to as field training. Police field training officers are referred to as FTOs and correctional training officers are referred to as CTOs. The length and extent of each field training process will vary from agency to agency depending upon size, responsibilities, and duties. Each of the field training phases discussed next are consistent with programs commonly found in medium to large police agencies. In smaller agencies, there may be abbreviated versions of these common field training processes.

Chapter 6 - Police Field Training

Throughout your first year of employment and during the field training process, you are referred to as a "probationary officer." You will be trained and evaluated by a field training officer (FTO). Ideally, the FTO is considered one of the agency's best and well trained officers and has received specialized training in coaching, teaching and evaluating probationary officers.

A typical police field training program consists of four phases, which may be shorter in duration in smaller agencies. During the first three phases, you will be assigned to three different FTOs for a minimum of four weeks each. During each phase you are progressively responsible for completing more of the daily workload. Phase four is commonly referred to as the "Shadow Phase" and the final step before you are qualified for solo patrol. During this final phase you will be reassigned to your first FTO. This allows the first FTO to see the progress you've made over the many weeks of training. Your initial FTO is in the best position to determine whether you're qualified for solo patrol. Each phase of the FTO program is further explained below.

Phase 1: This is the most basic phase of the field training process. It typically begins with you and your FTO getting all of your necessary paperwork in order. As the weeks progress, you may first watch your FTO handle basic calls for service (e.g., civil matters, simple thefts, or noise complaints) or simple police functions (e.g., traffic stops or traffic control) and then he/she will have you handle them. Based upon how well you progress, you may begin to advance to more complex calls for service. During this phase, you are typically responsible for five percent at the beginning of the phase to 25 percent of the daily workload at the end.

Phase 2: During this phase you will be assigned to another shift and a new FTO. You will be responsible for more of the workload (25 to 50 percent) and more advanced calls for service (e.g., operating while intoxicated stops, burglary cases, and domestic violence incidents). The workload percentages may increase if you are advancing at an above-average pace.

Phase 3: During this final phase of riding with a uniformed FTO, you will be assigned to yet another shift and a new FTO. You will be expected to handle a minimum of 50 percent of the workload at the beginning of the phase and nearly 100 percent by the end. You will also be expected to have demonstrated success in handling all previous calls for service in addition to more advanced and high-risk calls, such as armed robberies, crimes in progress, and weapons-related calls. Near the end of the phase, your FTO will make a recommendation or conclude that you are prepared to progress to Phase 4, the last step before solo patrol.

Phase 4: During this "shadow phase," you'll be in full uniform, while your FTO will be riding along with you, but not in uniform. During police-citizen interactions, people interact with the uniformed officer before the plainclothes FTO. This allows the FTO to evaluate how you handle calls for service from beginning to end. You are expected to handle 100 percent of the workload. Since your FTO is merely a shadow, you cannot rely on him/her for assistance, except in emergency situations. Otherwise, you are to function as though your FTO were not present and, if necessary, request backup, a supervisor, or for other resources necessary to properly handle the call for service. If you demonstrate competency during this phase, you are deemed qualified for solo patrol and will then be assigned to your regular shift assignment.

Each agency determines the approach to evaluation. It used to be common for agencies to use a rating scale with 1 being failing or unable to perform the essential duties and 5 meaning "exceeding standards." It is more common for agencies to use a simpler rating scale with only three measures: Does Not Meet Standards, Meets Standards, and Exceeds Standards. If you are performing well, it is most common that you will receive a "Meets Standards" evaluation and the "Exceeds Standards" rating identifies exemplary work. If you are receiving "Meets Standards" ratings, you have nothing to worry about and are successfully progressing through the program. The "Does Not Meet Standards" rating is typically given when you have failed to perform a task in the field that has been explained and demonstrated to you before you attempted to perform it. Mistakes are expected when you attempt a task for the first time and that is part of learning. However, if after numerous repetitions (approximately three attempts) of the FTO explaining and demonstrating a task, you fail to properly perform it, a "Does Not Meet Standards" rating will likely be documented. A pattern of these ratings is cause for concern and additional training may be required. You should make every effort to avoid "Does Not Meet Standards" ratings through diligent study of training materials provided by your agency, regularly seeking clarification of task and performance expectations, and constantly studying geography. Remember, if you cannot get to a call safely, you are of no use to anyone needing your assistance.

At the end of each week of training, you'll meet with a Field Training Supervisor (FTS) who has been assigned to oversee your training. Prior to this meeting, the FTS will first meet with your FTO to discuss the previous week of training. This is the opportunity for the FTO to share any training concerns with the FTS. The FTS will then meet with you, without your FTO present, which gives you the opportunity to speak freely regarding the previous week of training. This is also the best moment for you to share any concerns that you have related to your FTO. In some cases, there can be a personality conflict between you and your FTO. Let's face it, there can be conflicting personalities in any training environment, which can make communication and training that much more challenging. If you sense personality conflicts, this is the best time to bring it up. It may merely be a matter of perception and differences can be aired out and resolved. On the other hand, it may be a personality conflict that cannot be overcome, for whatever reason, and a new FTO could be assigned, although this happens rarely. It is expected that you will make all efforts to adjust your communications skills and personality traits to conform to your work environment.

The field training experience is stressful by design and it's imperative that you arrive for your shift prepared and ready to go. You will be evaluated on all aspects of police work, including operation of a marked squad car, familiarity with the geography of the area, application of written and verbal communications skills, use of tactical and radio communications skills, and the application of criminal and traffic laws. Oftentimes, learning the geography of the assigned area can be very challenging for new officers. After all, if you can't get to a call for service or officer needs assistance request, then you are not performing up to standard. You can reduce this unnecessary stress by driving around in the community or to random streets on your off time. Many officers before you have discovered that minimal performance, such as showing up for work and only putting in eight hours, is not enough to succeed in field training. Often you must demonstrate competency and proficiency in more than 20 essential tasks. Some of these tasks include:

- Children crimes
- Bank robbery
- Traffic stops
- OWI enforcement
- Crimes against property
- Crimes against persons
- High risk weapon calls
- High risk traffic stops
- Alarms
- Domestic disturbances
- Hostage situations
- Drug enforcement
- Sex crimes
- Retail theft

You must invest your own time to study and prepare, even on your off days, to ensure success. The more familiar you can become with the geographic area, the less stress you will have in this regard during field training. Officers who are more comfortable with geography spend less time worrying about how to get to a call for service and more time preparing to handle the call while on their way to the scene. Remember, the FTO is watching, documenting, and evaluating everything you do. If you cannot perform the essential functions of patrol work in the field training environment, and then in the position you've worked so hard to obtain, you will likely be terminated.

Correctional Officer Field Training Phases

Correctional officer field training programs are similar to the law enforcement FTO programs covered in this chapter. As a new correctional officer, you will be assigned to a CTO for your first phase of training. The CTO program normally has four phases of training; during each phase the workload you are responsible for will continue to increase. As you move from one phase to the next, you will likely work different shifts within the facility with a different CTO assigned to you. One of the primary differences in most FTO and CTO programs is that during Phase 4, the CTO will remain in uniform and not in a plainclothes "shadow" role.

The categories of evaluation within the CTO program are also consistent with the FTO program, with the exception of motor vehicle operation and geography. New correctional officers are expected to demonstrate competency in all other areas, such as written and verbal communications skills, use of tactical and radio communications skills, and the application of criminal laws and institutional rules. Some of the essential tasks your CTO will teach you include the following:

- Offender rights and privileges
- Reports and log entries
- Technology or computer usage
- Key & tool control
- Emergency situations and procedures
- Contraband and searches
- Offender escort and transport
- Use of restraints
- Use of force
- Tier and unit checks (prisoner counts)
- Offender mail procedures
- Medical emergencies and services

Upon completion of the FTO or CTO program, you will be assigned to a shift and complete the remainder of your 12- or 18-month probationary period. Remember, just because you successfully passed FTO or CTO training, doesn't mean you can become lackadaisical. You must continue to focus on becoming proficient in all aspects of your work and *never stop learning*.

Conclusion

There are few occupations that put you in a position to really make a difference in the lives of others. Serving others as a police or correctional officer can be very rewarding. It can also be life-changing, sometimes for the better and other times for worse. It's a well-known fact that police or correctional work will change you physically, emotionally, and psychologically.

As you progress through your career you'll encounter difficulties and challenges, both professionally and personally. Successful police and correctional officers tend to have the following three things in order: faith, family, and friends. Successful officers also embrace the idea of lifelong learning, which helps them keep fresh and current with changes and developments in their field. Embrace change, be a professional at all times, and never stop learning. See Appendix C for recommended reading for additional insight about career survival, including the long-term psychological and physiological impact that police and correctional work can have upon you.

In the end, it is my sincere hope that this book will help you become a successful police or correctional officer and allow you to make a difference in the lives of others.

Appendix A - The Ethical Warrior: The Hunting Story

Jack E. Hoban, United States Marine Corps & Bruce Gourlie, U.S. Army

Robert L. Humphrey, an Iwo Jima Marine rifle platoon commander who worked for the State Department during the Cold War, had to resolve a conflict between the U.S. and an allied country in Asia Minor. The local people wanted the Americans to go home, while the Americans had a strategic interest in keeping the Cold War missile base. Humphrey discovered that many of the U.S. servicemen considered the locals to be "stupid, dumb, dirty, dishonest, untrustworthy, disloyal, cowardly, lazy, unsanitary, immoral, cruel, crazy, and downright subhuman."

Understandably, the local people's perception was that the Americans did not view them as equal human beings. Their opposition to the presence of the U.S. installation was based on the fact that they simply wanted to be treated with respect and dignity.

One day, as a diversion from his job, Humphrey decided to go hunting for wild boar with some personnel from the American embassy. They took a truck from the motor pool and headed out to the boondocks, stopping at a village to hire some local men to beat the brush and act as guides. This village was very poor. The huts were made of mud and there was no electricity or running water. The streets were unpaved dirt and the whole village smelled. The men looked surly and wore dirty clothes. The women covered their faces, and the children had runny noses and were dressed in rags.

One American in the truck said, "This place stinks."

Another said, "These people live just like animals."

Finally, a young air force man said, "Yeah, they got nothin' to live for; they may as well be dead."

Then, an old sergeant in the truck spoke up. He was the quiet type who never said much. In fact, except for his uniform, he kind of reminded you of one of the tough men in the village. He looked at the young airman and said, "You think they got nothin' to live for, do you? Well, if you are so sure, why don't you just take my knife, jump down off the back of this truck, and go try to kill one of them?"

Dead silence. Humphrey was amazed.

It was the first time that anyone had said anything that had actually silenced the negative talk about these local people. The sergeant went on to say, "I don't know either why they value their lives so much. Maybe it's those snotty nosed kids, or the women in the pantaloons. But whatever it is, they care about their lives and the lives of their loved ones, same as we Americans do. And if we don't stop talking bad about them, they will kick us out of this country!"

Humphrey asked him what we Americans, with all our wealth, could do to prove our belief in the peasants' equality despite their destitution. The sergeant answered, "You got to be brave enough to jump off the back of this truck, knee deep in the mud and sheep dung. You got to have the courage to walk through this village with a smile on your face. And when you see the smelliest, scariest looking peasant, you got to be able to look him in the face and let him know, just with your eyes, that you know he is a man who hurts like you do, and hopes like you do, and wants for his kids just like we all do. It is that way, or we lose."

The hunting story has immediate and strong emotional impact. We sympathize with those poor villagers, perhaps because most people naturally root for the "underdog."

Almost everyone understands the pain and anger that arise from disrespect. The people in that village weren't speaking out, but in their hearts each of them was saying: "Don't look down on me. You are my equal — my life and the lives of my loved ones are as important to me as yours are to you." Everyone in the truck suddenly understood two things. First, despite how worthless the villager's life might appear, no one would actually try to kill him because taking innocent human life is anathema to all moral people. Second, if attacked, the villager would have defended himself with all his might because he loved his life and the lives of his loved ones just as much as everyone else. At last, here was Humphrey's way to make the truth that "all men are created equal" truly self-evident.

Humphrey had great success relating this insight he called the "Life Value" to other military personnel at the U.S. base in formal presentations...

Reprinted with Permission

What does the "hunting story" tell you about your morals, values, and ethics? How can you use the "hunting story" when answering ethical or diversity-related questions?

Appendix B - Oral Interview Questions & Scenarios

All of the following oral interview questions come from actual law enforcement or correctional officer oral interview board experiences:

1. What have you done to prepare yourself for a position in law enforcement or corrections?
2. What experiences do you have to apply towards a career in law enforcement or corrections?
3. Explain how you have accepted criticism directed at yourself.
4. What specific abilities and experience do you have that allows you to implement your own decisions?
5. Why should we certify you (i.e. send you through the academy) as a police or correctional officer instead of another candidate?
6. What is the most important quality a person can possess to be a good police or correctional officer?
7. How do you feel about working with officers or members of the community who have different backgrounds, races, religious beliefs, etc.?
8. What future goals would you like to achieve as a police or correctional officer?
9. What would you do if you responded to a call and a good friend had to be arrested?
10. What would you do if you stopped the village/city/town president (mayor) for a traffic violation and he/she was under the influence of alcohol?
11. If you caught your partner stealing what would you do?
12. What are some areas you can improve to make yourself a better candidate?
13. Where do you see yourself in your 5th year of law enforcement or corrections?
14. What are the major goals of a police department?
15. How do you feel about working with minorities? Tell us your definition of diversity and provide us with an example of how you have interacted with diverse populations. Give a specific example of a stressful situation that you have been in and how you handled it.
16. Provide an example of when you have demonstrated that you can work as part of a team.
17. Why do you want to become a police officer for the city, village, or town of _____?
18. Why do you want to become a correctional officer for the county or state of _____?
19. Explain what community policing means to you and how you would apply it in the field.
20. Explain the justification that is necessary for an officer to use deadly force.
21. Explain a time when you used appropriate empathy to help another person.
22. What are your objectives (i.e. goals) in police work and how can the department help you achieve them?
23. Have you ever taken advantage of an employer and/or know somebody who did? If so, what did you do and/or do about it?
24. How do you handle an ethical dilemma when you're faced with one?
25. Explain to us the daily duties of a police or correctional officer with "X" agency.
26. Provide us with an example of a time when you used communications skills to solve a problem in a work setting.

27. Provide us with an example of a time when you implemented a decision that people disagreed with.
28. What would you do if an offender or prisoner told you that you had nice hair and your perfume smelled nice? (This question is typically directed towards female candidates)
29. Tell us a time in your life when you got somebody to cooperate with you.
30. Describe a hurdle that you have overcome and how you overcame it
31. How does the [police or correctional agency/position] fit into your career goals?
32. You are on duty and see your co-worker doing something unethical. How would you handle it?
33. Tell us about a time when you worked individually and as a team to accomplish a goal and what your role in it was.
34. Tell us a time when a manager was not on duty and you had to make a decision and how you handled that decision.
35. Tell us about a time when you had to change your normal routine (or practice) and how you handled it.

Oral Interview Scenarios

Oral interview scenario questions will typically fall within two dimensions: tactical or ethical. Sometimes a scenario will include elements of both dimensions.

1. ETHICS-RELATED SCENARIO: You are a new police officer and you're with your FTO. You are called to back up another officer in a park where he is dealing with an intoxicated homeless person. While you're at the scene you observe the officer yell and kick the homeless person telling him to "get out of here." While the homeless person gets up to leave the officer continues to kick the subject and he falls to the pavement, cracks his head open, gets up, and staggers away. Your FTO says, "If anybody asks you about this, you didn't see anything." What would you response be?

2. TACTICAL RELATED SCENARIO: It is 3:00 p.m. and you and another officer are dispatched to a bank alarm. While en route, dispatch advises that the bank provided the proper code, but you still continue your response to confirm that all is okay. You arrive first and park at a corner of the bank. An armed gunman exits the bank with a hostage, sees your marked squad, pushes the hostage away, and keeps the gun at his side and screams, "kill me." What would your immediate actions/response be?

3. TACTICAL RELATED SCENARIO: It is 5:00 p.m. and you are involved in a high-speed chase of a stolen vehicle. Traffic conditions are heavy, but agency policy permits you to chase unless a supervisor advises you to terminate. As you enter a busy intersection, the stolen vehicle strikes another vehicle causing it to spin out and hit a traffic control signal, knocking it down. The victim vehicle is disabled and suffers considerable damage. The stolen vehicle continues to flee away from the scene. What would your immediate actions be?

4. ETHICS-RELATED SCENARIO: You are dispatched to a residence for a domestic violence complaint. Upon arrival, you realize the victim is a friend from high school. He reports that his wife punched him in the face and tipped over furniture before she left the house. Furniture is tipped over and there is a small cut on his left cheek. How would you handle that situation?

Appendix C: Recommended Reading

Gilmartin, Kevin M. *Emotional Survival for Law Enforcement: A Guide for Officers and Their Families*. Tucson, Ariz.: E-S Press, 2002.

Grossman, Dave, and Loren W. Christensen. *On Combat: The Psychology and Physiology of Deadly Conflict in War and in Peace*. 3rd ed. Illinois: Warrior Science Pub., 2008.

Grossman, Dave. *On Killing: The Psychological Cost of Learning to Kill in War and Society*. Rev. ed. New York: Little, Brown and Co., 2009.

Hoban, Jack. *The Ethical Warrior: Values, Morals & Ethics for Life, Work and Service*. Spring Lake, NJ: RGI Media and Publications, 2012.

Pressfield, Steven. *The Warrior Ethos*. Los Angeles: Black Irish Entertainment, 2011.

Shusko, Joseph C. *Tie-ins for Life*. Spring Lake, NJ: RGI Media & Publications, 2011.

Resources/Bibliography

Dantzker, M.L. (2011) *Psychological Preemployment Screening for Police Candidates: Seeking Consistency If Not Standardization.* American Psychological Association, 1 Jan. 2011. Retrieved from: http://www.google.com/url?sa=t&rct=j&q=&esrc=s&source=web&cd=1&ved=0CCMQFjAA&url=http://www.apa.org/pubs/journals/features/pro-42-3-276.pdf&ei=DE56VInNOJbbsASTuYLYCA&usg=AFQjCNGnm8ntBT7jceFhkDYsHcC5TWXuKw&bvm=bv.80642063,d.cWc&cad=rja

Goudreau, J. (2012, December 13). *How to land a new job in 2013.* Retrieved from http://www.forbes.com/sites/jennagoudreau/2012/12/13/how-to-get-a-new-job-in-2013/

Miller, Laurence (2007, July 16). *How to pass your pre-employment psych screening without going nuts.* Retrieved from: http://www.policeone.com/police-products/human-resources/articles/1282462-How-to-pass-your-pre-employment-psych-screening-without-going-nuts/

Occupational employment statistics. (2012). Retrieved from http://www.bls.gov/oes/current/oes333012.htm

Occupational employment statistics. (2012). Retrieved from http://www.bls.gov/oes/current/oes333051.htm

Roufa, Timothy (n.d.). *Psychological Exams and Screening for Police Officers.* Retrieved from: http://criminologycareers.about.com/od/Job_Market/a/Psychological-Screening-For-Police-Officers.htm

Smith, A. (2012, April 5). The GI bill is back, helping thousands of veterans. Retrieved from http://money.cnn.com/2012/04/05/news/economy/gi-bill-veterans/.

33339504R10050

Made in the USA
San Bernardino, CA
30 April 2016